Empower
Your Job Search
with AI Chatbots

Empower Your Job Search with AI Chatbots

136 Artificial Intelligence Prompts for Career Self-Help, Job Search Motivation, and Job Hunting Strategies

Mindscape Artwork Publishing
Vanessa Olcese
Mauricio Vasquez

Toronto, Canada

Authors:

Vanessa Olcese
Mauricio Vasquez

First Printing: February 2024

ISBN-978-1-998402-00-7 (Paperback)

ISBN-978-1-998402-02-1 (Hardcover)

DEDICATION

To those yearning for a brighter future and fulfilling career: May this book serve as your compass, guiding you through challenges and illuminating your path to success. Your dreams are valid; your efforts, noble. Reach for the stars.

Scan the QR code to access our book collection.

TABLE OF CONTENTS

INTRODUCTION

Welcome to a transformative journey led by Vanessa Olcese, a distinguished marketing professional in the tech world, and Mauricio Vasquez, an expert in Risk Management with a passion for Generative AI. Both have navigated surprising twists in their career paths. Their collective insights serve as the foundation for this guide, offering a fresh perspective on the job search process. While Vanessa and Mauricio hail from distinct professional backgrounds, their shared experience of navigating the volatile job market unites their stories, illustrating the shifting realities many face today.

In the ever-evolving world of work, the unexpected can become the expected overnight. Vanessa Olcese's story begins in the vast expanse of the tech industry, where after nearly two decades of serving a single company, she suddenly found herself on a path she never thought she'd tread: the job search. For Vanessa, the world had shifted. She had not had to navigate the treacherous waters of job hunting since her college days—days when she was handpicked from the crowd and steadily moved up the ladder of success. The very idea of starting from scratch, of putting herself out there in a vastly different job market, was overwhelming, to say the least.

But like all challenges, this one came with its own set of hidden treasures. Vanessa discovered an entirely new dimension to job searching—one that was powered by the marvels of Generative AI. This tool, previously unknown to her, transformed her journey from a daunting task into an adventure filled with insights and possibilities.

On the flip side, let's meet Mauricio Vasquez. Like many, Mauricio faced the abrupt jolt of unemployment after dedicating over two decades to the corporate sector. In 2020, as COVID-19 drastically altered the global landscape, his role was unexpectedly terminated, plunging him into a whirlpool of uncertainty.

However, Mauricio's journey diverged from Vanessa's. Initially, he grappled with conventional job search methods that were prevalent at the time. But today, Mauricio is equipped with a unique skill set. His deep understanding of prompt engineering and Generative AI not only enables him to guide others in their job hunts but also empowers him to use these innovative technologies for exploring new dimensions in career advancement.

This book is a confluence of two personal journeys—of discovery, resilience, and the unyielding spirit of pushing boundaries. Through these pages, Vanessa and Mauricio unravel the potent force of Generative AI and the magic of crafted prompts to supercharge one's job search. From those who are dipping their toes in the job market for the first time, to seasoned professionals facing unprecedented challenges, this guide serves as a beacon, illuminating a path towards success and fulfillment.

Our aim is not just to introduce you to a tool, but to redefine the very essence of job searching—to transform it from a process marred by anxiety and doubt to an empowering journey of growth and endless possibilities. So, whether you're just beginning, recalibrating, or looking for a fresh perspective, this book is your compass, ready to navigate you to your next professional horizon.

Let's embark on this journey together and unlock the doors that Generative AI can open for you.

Welcome to the future of job searching. Welcome to hope, empowerment, and boundless opportunity.

ABOUT THE AUTHORS

Vanessa Olcese is a seasoned marketing and sales leader with over 15 years of experience in the technology industry, primarily at Microsoft. Specializing in sales and marketing strategies for both Commercial and Consumer sectors, Vanessa has a proven track record of driving innovation, growth, and brand impact at scale. Her expertise spans across various domains including Sales & Marketing, Change Management, Leadership, Cloud Solutions, Cybersecurity, and Artificial Intelligence, making her a versatile leader in the tech space.

Vanessa is certified in Generative AI by Microsoft and LinkedIn and holds a Professional Diploma in Digital Marketing. Fluent in both English and Spanish, she has led cross-functional teams, focusing on sales, demand generation, pipeline acceleration, and business transformation. Recognized as a Festival of Media judge in 2020 and 2022, Vanessa is an energetic, passionate, and committed leader who excels in problem-solving and team collaboration. She holds a Bachelor's degree in International Business and Marketing from Florida International University.

If you want to connect with Vanessa, go to this link
https://www.linkedin.com/in/vanessaolcese or scan this QR code:

Mauricio Vasquez is a multifaceted professional with over 20 years of experience in risk management and insurance, specializing in sectors like mining, power, and renewable energy. He holds an Industrial Engineering degree, a Master's in Business Administration, and a Master's in Marketing and Commercial Management, along with certifications in Enterprise Risk Management and Artificial Intelligence.

Mauricio is also a certified Adler Trained Coach and a self-published author, focusing on personal growth and professional development. His expertise in Artificial Intelligence and Large Language Models Prompt engineering adds a unique layer to his professional background. Fluent in both English and Spanish, Mauricio has worked across Canada, the U.S., Latin America, and the Caribbean. In addition to his corporate roles, he is a Professional and Life Coach, committed to helping immigrants transition successfully to new lives in Canada. His approach is deeply rooted in building long-term relationships and providing tailored, impactful solutions to clients.

If you want to connect with Mauricio, go to this link
https://www.linkedin.com/in/mauriciovasquez or scan this QR code:

WHAT ARE NATURAL LANGUAGE PROCESSING CHATBOTS?

An Artificial Intelligence [AI] Chatbot is a program within a website or app that uses machine learning [ML] and natural language processing [NLP] to interpret inputs and understand the intent behind a request or "prompt" [more on this later in the book]. Chatbots can be rule-based with simple use cases or more advanced and able to handle multiple conversations.

The rise of language models like GPT has revolutionized the landscape of conversational AI. These Chatbots now boast advanced capabilities that can mimic not just a human conversation style but also a [super] human mind. They can find information online and produce unique content and insights.

The most important thing to know about an AI Chatbot is that it combines ML and NLP to understand what people need and bring the best answers. Some AI Chatbots are better for personal use, like conducting research, and others are best for business use, like featuring a Chatbot on your company's website.

With this in mind, we've compiled a list of the best AI Chatbots for job search at the time of the writing of this book. We strongly suggest that you try and test each of the most popular ones and see what works best for you.

ChatGPT:
- Uses NLP to understand the context of conversations to provide related and original responses in a human-like conversation.
- Multiple use cases for things like answering questions, ideating and getting inspiration, or generating new content [like a marketing email].
- Improves over time as it has more conversations.

Bing Chat:
- Uses NLP and ML to understand conversation prompts.
- The compose feature can generate original written content and images, and its powerful search engine capabilities can surface answers from the web.
- It's a conversational tool, so you can continue sending messages until you're satisfied.

Google Bard:
- Google's Bard is a multi-use AI Chatbot.
- It's powered by Google's LaMDA [instead of GPT].
- Use it for things like brainstorming and ideation, drafting unique and original content, or getting answers to your questions.
- Connected to Google's website index so it can access information from the internet.

Meta LLaMa:
- Meta's Chatbot is an open source large language [LLM].
- The tool is trained using reinforcement learning from human feedback [RLHF], learning from the preferences and ratings of human AI trainers.

Starting from now, we will refer to these platforms as Chatbots. For a comprehensive guide on how to sign up to each, please refer to Appendix No 1. As of the book's publication date, the information herein is current and accurate. The Chatbot industry, however, is dynamic, with constant updates and new entrants. While specifics may evolve, our prompts, core strategies and principles discussed in this book are designed to withstand the test of time, offering you a robust framework for navigating this fast-paced landscape.

THE BENEFITS OF USING AI CHATBOTS IN YOUR JOB SEARCH

In today's competitive market, the job search can feel like a job within itself. Some people submit dozens of applications each week throughout their search. And not only are they doing that, but to stand out amongst a sea of applicants, it's also vital to customize job search assets.

But who has the time for that? None of us did before Chatbots, but the game has changed with their arrival. Chatbots are an incredible tool, and when used correctly, it can significantly help job seekers reach their career goals even faster and better.

Based on a survey conducted in February 2023 by ResumeBuilder.com, which included 1,000 individuals currently seeking employment or who had recently sought employment, it was found that approximately 46% of job seekers are utilizing Chatbots to create their resumes or cover letters.

74% of respondents saw a higher response rate from companies when using Chatbots. 78% of candidates who used the Chatbot scored interviews, while nearly 60% of job hunters were hired after using an AI tool during their application process. However, it is worth mentioning that 11% of job seekers were rejected once it was learned from the hiring company that the candidate used them. Please keep this in mind to avoid a similar outcome for you.

These findings shed light on the dynamic landscape of job hunting, as well as the ever-expanding role of cutting-edge technologies. With Chatbots seamlessly integrating into the fabric of the job application process, job seekers are presented with a powerful ally that empowers them to curate persuasive and compelling resumes or cover letters, for example.

Such an alliance fosters an environment where candidates can harness the creative potential of artificial intelligence to stand out from the crowd and find the right job faster and with less effort.

Here are 5 key benefits of leveraging this book with Chatbots throughout your job search process:

1. **FAST SPEED:** Chatbots can save you significant time when applying for jobs. Not only can it help you quickly create a compelling cover letter, but it can also help you apply for jobs, prepare for a job interview, and even generate a resume in record time.

2. **HIGH QUALITY:** Job search assets generated by Chatbots will never be 100% perfect—but they're a great starting point. So long as you're giving the best possible prompts and direction, you can generate cover letters and resumes highlighting the most important skills and metrics for the roles you're applying to. Job search assets are documents and resources used to showcase your skills, experience, and qualifications to potential employers.

3. **CUTTING EDGE:** A surefire way to stand out in a crowded job market is by customizing your resume and cover letter for each role you apply to. Very few job seekers are doing this, allowing the ones who actually do it to have the opportunity to stand out. But when you're applying to many roles, you need a way to do this at scale. Tailoring your resume to focus on the relevant skills for a specific job demonstrates your understanding of what the potential employer is looking for and can enhance your chances of getting the job.

4. **INNOVATIVE INSPIRATION:** Not only can Chatbots help you generate personalized cover letters and resumes, but it can also help you get inspiration for them too. With the help of valuable prompts, you can ask to show you successful job search assets in your industry and create templates that you can use for each job application you submit.

5. **SELF-WORTH BOOST:** This book's role as a supportive tool is to empower job seekers. It helps them remind themselves of their unique value and competencies, preparing them to navigate job search challenges and seize opportunities. By leveraging Chatbots in conjunction with this book, job seekers can gain personalized guidance and insights, boosting their self-worth and equipping them for success in their job search journey.

WHAT ARE PROMPTS?

Imagine stepping into a high-stakes negotiation with only half the information—you're likely to miss the mark. Similarly, Chatbots rely on well-crafted prompts to deliver precise and valuable responses.

Prompts serve as the guiding questions, suggestions, or ideas that instruct Chatbots on how and what to respond. But these aren't just any text or phrase; prompts are carefully engineered inputs designed to optimize the Chatbot's output for quality, relevance, and accuracy.

Prompts are suggestions, questions, or ideas for what Chatbots should respond. And for Chatbots to provide a helpful response to its user, they need a thorough prompt with some background information and relevant data. Becoming a solid prompt writer takes time and experience, but there are also some best practices that you can use to see success fairly quickly:

1. **Be specific:** When using Chatbots it's important to be as specific as possible. Being specific can include tone suggestions as well as length. You should also help Chatbots be really clear on what it's creating and how it can be impactful. For example, *"Write me a cover letter in a persuasive tone for X role at Y company. This cover letter should be engaging to read and focus on my experience in A, B, and C. Please keep the cover letter to no more than 250 words. Use short paragraphs."*

2. **Provide context:** While the above prompt is extremely helpful, it's missing one core component: context. And luckily, context is very easy to incorporate. You could still use most of the prompt above; you'd just also ask to skim a job description and resume that you'd paste underneath your prompt and use those resources to shape the final product. That way, Chatbots could create a cover letter that's really specific to you and the role you're applying for. We'll share over 100 prompts with some added context within this book.

3. **Use multiple prompts:** Using multiple prompts is a great way to get comfortable with Chatbots and the answers it provides. It's also great for job search assets, like resumes, with multiple sections and requirements. You can use each prompt to mold a new section of your assets. For example, *"Write me a cover letter opening paragraph for the content strategist role a Spotify using the job description below as a reference. Ensure the introduction packs a punch and will engage the reader immediately."*

4. **Always refine:** While Chatbots can be a beneficial tool for more job applicants in their search, it should never be taken at face value and always be enhanced with the applicant's own perspective and voice. The results are meant to provide suggestions—not be copied and pasted word-for-word. Think of these cover letter prompts as a supplement to your own thoughts and ideas, not an exact replacement.

5. **Use follow-up prompts:** Utilize follow-up prompts to enhance Chatbot performance. Build the next prompt based on the Chatbot's previous response to maintain conversational flow and improve answer accuracy. For example, follow "*Tell me about the best practices for email marketing*" with "*What are the pros and cons of each strategy?*" This approach ensures more focused and relevant dialogue.

   Check Appendix No 2 for 100 follow-up prompts you could use, but remember they also need to be tailored to the specific conversation you are having with the Chatbot.

HOW TO USE THIS BOOK?

Navigating the job search landscape has never been more complex, yet ripe with opportunities for those who know how to leverage cutting-edge technologies. This book serves as a comprehensive guide to harnessing the power of Chatbots in your job search journey. While the chapters are organized to mirror the traditional phases of job-seeking, this book is designed for nonlinear consumption. Feel free to dive into the sections that resonate most with your current needs.

- **Optimize Your Job Search Outcomes with Our Specialized GPT:** We are excited to offer you exclusive access to "CAREER NAVIGATOR AI" GPT, an advanced tool developed using OpenAI's ChatGPT technology, specifically tailored for the job search process. This innovative GPT model is designed to provide you with targeted assistance in navigating the complexities of job searching, enhancing your career path with AI-driven insights. To maximize its impact, we recommend using "CAREER NAVIGATOR AI" in conjunction with the prompts provided in this book. To access this GPT, please refer to the following chapter in this book.

- **Prompt Engineering for Optimal Outcomes:** We advocate for an informed, strategic approach to using the prompts provided in this book. Each prompt is meticulously engineered to serve a specific purpose and is accompanied by its intended goal, a guiding formula, and two illustrative examples. Text highlighted in **bold** and terms enclosed in square brackets **[ ]** are particularly conducive to customization. We encourage you to not just copy these prompts verbatim but to understand their underlying structure and adapt them to your unique circumstances. The more tailored the prompt, the more relevant and actionable the output will be.

- **Multi-Modal Strategies for Customization:** Feel free to mix and match elements from different formulas to create prompts that are uniquely suited to your objectives. The quality of the prompts you use is directly proportional to the quality of the responses you'll receive. Therefore, investing time in fine-tuning your prompts is not just recommended; it's essential.

- **Ethical and Responsible Use of AI:** While Chatbots offers a wealth of information and insights, it's crucial to approach its advice with a critical mindset. Use the responses as a starting point and build upon them through further research and reflection. Always remember that while AI can be a powerful tool, it is not infallible and should not replace human judgment.

- **Communication Best Practices:** When interacting with Chatbots, aim for a conversational tone and avoid jargon or overly complex phrases. Open-ended questions are more likely to yield detailed and insightful answers, so steer clear of yes-or-no queries. You can also set a persona for Chatbots to assume, providing a unique lens through which the AI can offer advice.

- **Audience and Context:** Define the audience or industry for whom you'll be using the insights garnered from Chatbots. Whether it's for personal use, a specific job application, or broader career planning, having a clear audience in mind will help you tailor your prompts more effectively.

- **Documentation and Continuous Learning:** We recommend documenting your interactions and insights about your job search in a dedicated notebook. This practice not only enhances memory retention but also allows for ongoing refinement. Check Appendix No 3 for FREE RESOURCES of a productivity planner, habit tracker, job search and more to help you with your job search.

- **ChatGPT Plugins for Enhanced Functionality:** Utilize specialized ChatGPT plugins to streamline your job search. These plugins can automate tasks like resume parsing, job board scraping, and interview preparation, offering a more integrated and efficient approach to landing your ideal job. Check Appendix No 4 for more information about ChatGPT plugins.

- **Third-Party Tools for Augmented Job Search:** This section curates a selection of external platforms aimed at enriching your job search. While we don't have affiliations with these resources, we can't vouch for their reliability or accuracy. Exercise due diligence when leveraging these platforms for your job search. Check Appendix No 5.

- **Introduction to ChatGPT:** Appendix No 6 contains a step-by-step guide to walk you through the this platform, empowering you to leverage its capabilities for an enhanced job search experience and more.

- **'Career Navigator AI' GPT Integration**: Access our exclusive 'Career Navigator AI' GPT, powered by OpenAI's ChatGPT, for personalized, AI-driven career advice. This tool offers interactive support in resume crafting, interview prep, and understanding job market trends. Utilize it for a tailored approach to your job search. See Appendix No 7 for details and access to this tool.

The job search process is an evolving journey, and this book aims to make that journey more informed, strategic, and successful. By understanding the intricacies of prompt engineering and responsibly leveraging AI, you can significantly enhance the quality of your job search and, ultimately, your career trajectory.

MEET THE "CAREER NAVIGATOR AI" GPT

The **"CAREER NAVIGATOR AI"** GPT, developed using OpenAI's ChatGPT technology, revolutionizes your job search experience by offering a highly tailored and responsive interaction.

This custom GPT (Generative Pre-trained Transformer) model has been meticulously crafted to provide focused assistance in the areas of job search, career planning, and interview preparation.

As a dynamic Artificial Intelligence companion, it aligns with your unique career aspirations and needs, offering personalized advice and insights to help you navigate the complexities of the job market. Engaging with this GPT is incredibly intuitive and simpler than you might expect. Once you access ChatGPT, you'll be greeted by a user-friendly interface where you can input your job search queries or prompts.

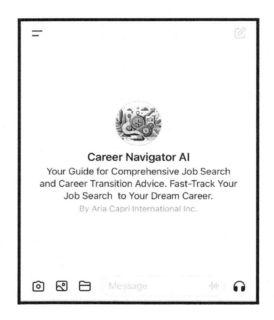

The GPT responds almost instantly, offering valuable insights and practical guidance to enhance your job search strategy. Whether you aim to refine your resume, prepare for interviews, or identify the best career paths, the "CAREER NAVIGATOR AI" GPT is your gateway to a more effective and innovative job search process.

Included in this section there are two screenshots showing the user interface you'll encounter when accessing the 'CAREER NAVIGATOR AI' GPT. This visual guide provides a clear overview of what to expect, easing your first steps in leveraging this cutting-edge tool.

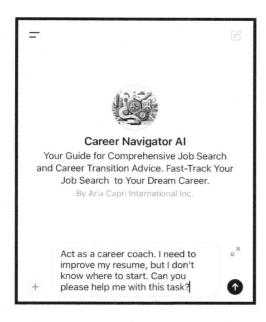
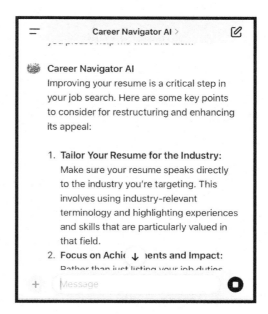

To embark on your journey towards a successful career and to experience this unique blend of knowledge and technology, please scan this QR code:

Disclaimer: There's a monthly fee for using OpenAI's Plus plan, which you need to access the GPT I created for this book. Wanted to be clear – I don't get any income from OpenAI for suggesting their service. It's all about giving you great tools, and that's why I produced this GPT specifically for the book and for you. As of now, us GPT builders don't get a share of OpenAI's earnings, but if that ever changes – I'll update the disclaimer right away. Mauricio

FREE GOODWILL

Would you be willing to make a small gesture with a lasting impact? One that doesn't cost a dime and takes less than a minute?

Consider this: right now, there's someone out there striving to find a new job, better support their family, and navigate the complexities of the job market. Just like you, they're seeking guidance. Your feedback on this book can be the beacon they need.

Reviews are more than just feedback—they're recommendations, shared wisdom, and signs of trust. If this book provides you with valuable insights, could you take a moment to share your thoughts with a brief review? Your words have the power to:

- Guide someone toward their dream job.
- Enable an individual to better support their loved ones.
- Offer a transformative experience someone might have missed.
- Inspire positive change in another's life.
- By leaving a review, you become part of someone else's success story. And if this book resonates with you, consider sharing it. When you introduce someone to a valuable resource, they'll remember the kind gesture.

From the depths of our hearts, thank you for being a beacon of hope and guidance.

Warmly,

Vanessa & Mauricio

PS. To leave your kind review, please scan this QR code.

JOB SEARCH PROMPTS

1. PUTTING YOUR FINANCIAL HOUSE IN ORDER

This chapter stands as your guide through the often tricky business of managing money while looking for a job or shifting careers. It's packed with prompts that mimic the kind of smart advice you'd get from a top-notch financial advisor, tailored just for you. These aren't just prompts—they're smart tips to help you keep a tight rein on your budget, save wisely, and be ready for anything money-wise.

As you turn these pages, you'll find clear steps to sort out any money matter, from chatting about finances with your family to getting a handle on debts, or even investing in yourself without going over budget. Every piece of advice here is about taking action and staying positive. It's about seeing financial planning as an exciting part of moving forward in your career, equipping you to not just get by but to really succeed.

PROMPT No. 1

Goal

To provide guidance on how to manage your finances effectively during your job search process.

Prompt

Act as a **financial advisor** specializing in **career transitions** for professionals in the **manufacturing industry**. What **strategies** can I adopt to **manage my finances effectively** during my **job-seeking journey**? Provide extensive and thorough **strategies**. Present non-traditional **strategies**. Write using a **positive** tone and **conversational** writing style. Let's think about this step by step.

Formula

Act as a **[profession]** specializing in **[topic]** for professionals in the **[industry]**. What **[strategies/tactics]** can I adopt to **[objective/outcome]** during my **[process/journey]**? Provide extensive and thorough **[strategies/tactics]**. Present non-traditional **[strategies/tactics]**. Write using a **[type]** tone and **[style]** writing style. Let's think about this step by step.

Examples

1. Act as a financial consultant specializing in saving strategies for professionals in the tech industry. What strategies can I adopt to maintain financial stability during my career transition? Provide extensive and thorough strategies. Present non-traditional strategies. Write using a motivated tone and technical writing style. Let's think about this step by step.
2. Act as a financial planner specializing in bankruptcies for professionals in the investment industry. What strategies can I adopt to manage my finances effectively while I'm seeking a new job? Provide extensive and thorough strategies. Present non-traditional strategies. Write using a professional tone and informative writing style. Let's think about this step by step.

PROMPT No. 2

Goal

To provide you with advice on budgeting during the job search process.

Prompt

Act as a **budgeting coach** specializing in **job transitions** for professionals in the **insurance industry**. How can I **create and maintain a budget** during **my job search** to **ensure financial stability**? Present detailed and broad-ranging solutions. Provide unique and overlooked solutions. Write using a **motivated** tone and **creative** writing style. Let's take this one step at a time.

Formula

Act as a **[profession]** specializing in **[topic]** for professionals in the **[industry]**. How can I **[action/behavior]** during my **[process/journey]** to **[objective/outcome]**? Present detailed and broad-ranging solutions. Provide unique and overlooked solutions. Write using a **[type]** tone and **[style]** writing style. Let's take this one step at a time.

Examples

1. Act as a budgeting expert specializing in job search for professionals in the tech industry. How can I manage my budget effectively during my job search? Present detailed and broad-ranging solutions. Provide unique and overlooked solutions. Write using an inspirational tone and creative writing style. Let's take this one step at a time.
2. Act as a financial coach specializing in debt restructuring for professionals in the tech sector. How can I come up with strategies to control my monthly budget during my job-seeking journey? Present detailed and broad-ranging strategies. Provide unique and overlooked strategies. Write using a motivated tone and technical writing style. Let's take this one step at a time.

PROMPT No. 3

Goal

To provide strategies for saving money during your job search process.

Prompt

Act as a **financial advisor** with a focus on **saving strategies** for professionals in the **education services industry**. What **strategies** can I adopt to **save money effectively** during my **job-seeking journey**? Share rare and lesser-known **strategies**. Offer in-depth and exhaustive **strategies**. Write using a **hopeful** tone and **descriptive** writing style. Let's address this point by point.

Formula

Act as a **[profession]** with a focus on **[topic]** for professionals in the **[industry]**. What **[strategies/tactics]** can I adopt to **[objective/outcome]** during my **[process/journey]**? Share rare and lesser-known **[strategies/tactics]**. Offer in-depth and exhaustive **[strategies/tactics]**. Write using a **[type]** tone and **[style]** writing style. Let's address this point by point.

Examples

1. Act as a personal finance coach with a focus on cost-saving measures for job seekers in the retail industry. What tactics can I adopt to save unnecessary expenses during my job search? Share rare and lesser-known tactics. Offer in-depth and exhaustive tactics. Write using an empathetic tone and descriptive writing style. Let's address this point by point.
2. Act as a financial planner with a focus on career transitions for professionals in the tourism sector. How can I manage my savings effectively during my job-seeking journey? Impart unconventional wisdom. Offer in-depth and exhaustive wisdom. Write using an upbeat tone and instructive writing style. Let's address this point by point.

PROMPT No. 4

To provide guidance on how you could handle financial stress during the job search process.

Prompt

Act as a **financial stress management coach** with a focus on **marriage relationships** for professionals in the **healthcare industry**. What **strategies** can I adopt to **manage financial stress** during my **job-seeking journey**? Deliver all-inclusive and extensive **strategies**. Propose novel **strategies**. Write using a **positive** tone and **constructive** style. Let's think about this step by step.

Formula

Act as a [profession] with a focus on **[topic]** for professionals in the **[industry]**. What **[strategies/solutions]** can I adopt to **[benefit/outcome]** during my **[process/journey]**? Deliver all-inclusive and extensive **[strategies/solutions]**. Propose novel **[strategies/solutions]**. Write using a **[type]** tone and **[style]** writing style. Let's think about this step by step.

Examples

1. Act as a financial wellness coach specializing in job transitions for professionals in the hospitality industry. What solutions can I adopt to manage financial stress during my job search? Deliver all-inclusive solutions. Propose novel solutions. Write using an empathetic tone and constructive writing style. Let's think about this step by step.
2. Act as a financial stress management expert with a focus on family therapy for professionals in the consumer packaged goods industry. What techniques can I use to handle financial challenges effectively with my family during my job-seeking journey? Deliver extensive techniques. Propose novel techniques. Write using an instructive tone and conversational writing style. Let's think about this step by step.

PROMPT No. 5

Goal

To provide guidance on how to plan for potential financial emergencies during the job search process.

Prompt

Act as a **financial planner** specializing in **managing emergency funds**. What strategies can I adopt to **plan for potential financial emergencies** during my **job-seeking journey**? Suggest **offbeat approaches** and **hidden gems**. Write using a **hopeful** tone and **critical** writing style. Let's dissect this carefully.

Formula

Act as a **[profession]** specializing in **[topic/industry]**. What strategies can I adopt [objective/outcome] during my [process/journey]? Suggest [tactics/aproaches] and **[tactics/suggestions]**. Write using a **[style]** tone and **[type]** writing style. Let's dissect this carefully.

Examples

1. Act as a financial advisor specializing in the tech industry. How can I build an emergency fund during my job search? Provide unique insights and overlooked opportunities. Write using a concise and critical writing style. Let's dissect this carefully.

2. Act as a financial planner specializing in estate planning. What strategies can I adopt to plan for unexpected expenses during my job-seeking journey? Share distinctive guidance and unexplored options. Write using an instructive and critical writing style. Let's unpack this topic.

PROMPT No. 6

Goal

To provide you with advice on how to communicate effectively about financial matters during the job search process.

Prompt

Act as a **financial communication coach** with a focus on **family health**. How can I **talk to my family about my financial situation** during my **job search in a way that fosters understanding and support**? Impart unique **suggestions** and undiscovered **possibilities**. Write using a **hopeful** tone and **reflective** writing style. Let's analyze this piece by piece.

Formula

Act as a **[profession]** with a focus on **[subject/topic]**. How can I **[benefit/outcome]** during my **[process/journey]**? Impart unique **[suggestions/tactics]** and undiscovered **[possibilities/tactics]**. Write using a [type] tone and **[style]** writing style. Let's analyze this piece by piece.

Examples

1. Act as a financial communication expert with a focus on financial crises. How can I discuss my financial situation during my job search with my partner in a way that fosters empathy and encouragement? Impart unique suggestions and undiscovered possibilities. Write using a hopeful tone and reflective writing style. Let's analyze this piece by piece.
2. Act as a financial relationship coach with a focus on financial literacy coaching. How can I communicate my financial challenges and successes during my job search to my family in a way that fosters mutual respect and support? Furnish a thorough and all-inclusive understanding. Write using a confident tone and reflective writing style. Let's unpack this topic.

PROMPT No. 7

Goal

To provide advice on managing debt while you look for a new job.

Prompt

Act as a **debt management coach** with a focus on **family financial distress**. What **action plans** can I implement to **manage my increasing debt effectively** during my **job-seeking journey**? Suggest **all-embracing and detailed action plans**. Provide separately traditional and nontraditional **action plans**. Write using a **concise** tone and **inspirational** writing style. Let's address this point by point.

Formula

Act as a **[profession]** with a focus on **[industry/topic]**. What **[action plans/strategies]** can I implement to [objective/outcome] during my **[process/journey]**? Suggest **[action plans/strategies]**. Provide separately traditional and nontraditional **[action plans/strategies]**. Write using a **[tone]** and **[style]** writing style. Let's address this point by point.

1. Act as a financial consultant with a focus on debt management. What strategies can I implement to keep my debt under control while I'm seeking a new job? Provide unique insights and overlooked opportunities. Provide separately traditional and nontraditional opportunities. Write using a concise tone and critical writing style. Let's go through this systematically.
2. Act as a debt management expert with a focus in the tax planning industry. What solutions can I develop to manage my debt effectively during my job search? Give atypical suggestions and unsung resources. Write using an empathetic tone and conversational writing style. Let's break this down into smaller parts.

PROMPT No. 8

Goal

To provide strategies for maintaining a good credit score during the job search process.

Prompt

Act as a **credit score coach** with a focus on **personal finance**. What **strategies** can I adopt **to maintain a good credit score** during my **job-seeking journey**? Present **non-traditional methods and underexplored resources**. Your response should be comprehensive, leaving no important aspect unaddressed. Write using a **confident** tone and **assertive** writing style. Let's dissect this carefully

Formula

Act as a **[profession]** with a focus on **[topic/subject]**. What **[strategies/action plans]** can I adopt to **[objective/outcome]** during my **[process/journey]**? Present **[method/strategies]** and **[resources/tactics]**. Your response should be comprehensive, leaving no important aspect unaddressed. Write using a **[tone]** and **[style]** writing style. Let's dissect this carefully

Examples

1. Act as a financial adviser with a focus on credit rehabilitation. What strategies can I adopt to improve my credit score during my job-seeking journey? Present unconventional credit repair techniques and underexplored resources. Your response should be comprehensive, leaving no important aspect unaddressed. Write using a confident tone and assertive writing style. Let's dissect this carefully.
2. Act as a personal finance consultant with a focus on debt management. How can I avoid damaging my credit score while managing my debts during my job-seeking journey? Present non-traditional debt handling strategies and less-known financial tools. Your response should be exhaustive, leaving no key detail untouched. Write using an authoritative tone and assertive writing style. Let's approach this methodically.

PROMPT No. 9

Goal

To provide guidance on how to make financially informed job decisions.

Prompt

Act as a **career and financial advisor** with a focus on **financial planning**. How can I **make financially informed decisions** when **evaluating job offers**? Share distinctive **guidance and**

unexplored options. Write using an inspirational tone and conversational writing style. Let's go through this systematically

Formula

Act as a **[profession]** with a focus on **[topic]**. How can I **[objective/outcome]** when **[situation]**? Share distinctive **[guidance/strategies]** and **[options/tactics]**. Write using an **[tone]** and **[style]** writing style. Let's go through this systematically.

Examples

1. Act as a personal finance consultant with a focus on budgeting. How can I budget my finances effectively to survive a period of unemployment? Suggest innovative methods and untapped resources. Write using an empathetic tone and straightforward writing style. Let's address this step by step.
2. Act as a financial health coach with a focus on saving strategies. What methods can I use to grow my savings during my job-seeking phase? Recommend unconventional approaches and rarely discussed strategies. Write using a motivational tone and clear writing style. Let's break this down systematically.

PROMPT No. 10

Goal

To provide advice on investing in yourself during the job search process.

Prompt

You are a **financial advisor** with a focus on **personal investment**. How can I **invest in myself effectively** during my **job-seeking journey** without **straining my finances**? Offer unconventional tips and lesser-known **ideas**. Write using an **empathetic** tone and **reflective** writing style. Let's analyze this piece by piece.

Formula

You are a **[profession]** with a focus on **[industry/topic]**. How can I **[objective/outcome]** during my **[process or application]** without **[outcome]**? Offer unconventional tips and lesser-known **[ideas/solutions]** . Write using a **[tone]** and **[style]** writing style. We should break this down into smaller parts.

Examples

1. You are a personal finance coach with a focus on professional development. How can I invest in my skills and career development during my job search without breaking the bank? Share distinctive guidance and unexplored options. Write using an empathetic tone and assertive writing style. Let's approach this gradually.
2. You are a financial planner with a focus on personal growth. How can I budget for personal and professional development expenses during my job-seeking journey? Offer unconventional tips and lesser-known options. Write using an instructive tone and engaging writing style. Let's address this point by point.

2. THE HEALTH DIMENSION

Embarking on a job search pushes not only your professional abilities but also your physical, mental, and emotional boundaries. In "The Health Dimension" chapter, we emphasize the pivotal role of health during this journey, offering strategies to promote resilience and disciplined health habits.

As you explore this chapter, envision each strategy as a tool, bolstering your body and mind against the challenges of job-seeking, and laying a robust foundation for your career aspirations.

PROMPT No. 11

Goal

To provide guidance on methods to improve your personal resilience in physical, mental, and emotional aspects during the challenging process of a job search.

Prompt

Assume the role of a **life coach** specializing in the **self-publishing industry**. What **strategies** can I adopt to **enhance** my **physical, mental, and emotional resilience** throughout **my job-seeking journey**? Include uncommon advice and underrated resources. Give comprehensive and detailed strategies. Write using a **hopeful** tone and **instructive** writing style. Let's approach this gradually.

Formula

Assume the role of a [profession] specializing in the [industry]. What [strategies/action plans] can I adopt to [benefit/outcome] my [characteristic/skill] throughout my [phase/process]? Include uncommon advice and underrated resources. Give comprehensive and detailed [strategies/action plans]. Write using a [tone] and [style] writing style. Let's dissect this carefully.

Examples

1. Assume the role of a wellness consultant specializing in the technology sector. What measures can I take to bolster my emotional fortitude throughout my career transition process? Include unconventional methods and overlooked tools. Provide an in-depth and complete set of recommendations. Write using an optimistic tone and guiding writing style. Let's embark on this journey step-by-step.
2. Assume the role of a mental strength coach with a focus on the entrepreneurial domain. What tactics can I utilize to strengthen my mental and, emotional resilience during my job-hunting journey? Incorporate rare insights and lesser-known resources. Offer thorough and extensive tactics. Write using an encouraging tone and instructional writing style. Let's take this one stage at a time.

PROMPT No 12

Goal

To underscore the importance and benefits of maintaining disciplined health habits during your job search periods and provide best practices to promote your well-being and resilience.

Prompt

I want you to act as a **wellness consultant** who specializes in the **construction industry**. Could you share the **advantages** of **maintaining disciplined health habits** during **the job-seeking phase**? Provide specific **best practices** I should consider. Offer unconventional **strategies** and underused

tools. Write using an instructive tone and descriptive writing style. Let's go through this systematically.

Formula

I want you to act as a **[profession]** who specializes in the **[industry]**. Could you share the **[attribute/descriptor]** of **[action/behavior]** during the **[phase/process]**? Provide specific **[best practices/tactics]** I should consider. Offer unconventional **[strategies/ideas]** and underused **[tools/resources]**. Write using a **[tone]** and **[style]** writing style. Let's go through this systematically.

Examples

1. I want you to act as a health coach who specializes in the tech industry. Could you elaborate on the benefits of sustaining regular exercise habits during the job-hunting period? Offer unique recommendations I should follow. Suggest innovative routines and lesser-known equipment. Write using a motivational tone and illustrative writing style. Let's dissect this carefully.
2. I want you to act as a nutritionist who specializes in the financial industry. Could you discuss the advantages of sticking to a balanced diet during the job transition phase? Provide specific dietary guidelines I should adhere to. Propose non-traditional meal plans and overlooked supplements. Write using an informative tone and precise writing style. Let's navigate this systematically.

PROMPT No. 13

Goal

To solicit valuable strategies for developing a balanced and efficient routine that contributes to your successful job search.

Prompt

You are a **wellness coordinator** with expertise in the **transportation industry**. Could you share some **effective strategies** for **establishing a healthy and productive routine for job searching**? Impart comprehensive and profound **information**, including rare wisdom and little-known insights. Write using a **positive** tone and **assertive** writing style. Let's take this one step at a time.

Formula

You are a **[profession]** with expertise in the **[industry]**. Could you share some **[quality/characteristic]** **[strategies/action plans]** for **[action/process]**? Impart comprehensive and profound **[information/response]**, including rare wisdom and little-known insights. Write using an **[tone]** and **[style]** writing style. Let's take this one step at a time.

Examples

1. Act as a time-management expert with a focus on the healthcare industry. Could you share some efficient methods for designing a balanced daily routine conducive to job searching? Furnish comprehensive and in-depth details, including overlooked strategies and niche tips. Write using an encouraging tone and confident writing style. Let's break this down progressively.
2. You are a productivity guru with specialization in the tech industry. Could you provide some practical steps to cultivate a consistent routine that optimizes job hunting efforts? Deliver thorough and substantial knowledge, featuring unconventional tactics and seldom-shared wisdom. Write using a positive tone and assertive writing style. Let's take this piece by piece.

Goal

To provide actionable suggestions to boost your physical, mental, and emotional well-being during the job search.

Prompt

Acting as a **wellness coach** who specializes in the **professional service industry**, provide me with **positive measures** I could consider to **improve my physical, mental, and emotional well-being**. Suggest offbeat approaches and hidden gems. Write using a **motivated** tone and **assertive** writing style. Let's take this one step at a time

Formula

Acting as a **[profession]** who specializes in the **[industry/topic]**, provide me with **[quality/characteristic] [tactics/strategies]** I could consider to **[objective/outcome]**? Give atypical suggestions and unsung resources. Write using a **[tone]** and **[style]** writing style. Let's address this point by point.

Examples

1. Taking on the role of a holistic wellness consultant focused on the technology industry, can you deliver insightful methods I could implement to bolster my physical, mental, and emotional well-being during a stressful job transition? Offer unconventional advice and lesser-known resources. Write with a confident and enthusiastic tone. Let's address this point by point.
2. As a mental health expert specializing in the creative industry, could you provide distinctive strategies I could adopt to fortify my emotional, mental, and physical well-being amidst job hunting? Propose non-mainstream approaches and overlooked tools. Write with a positive and assertive tone. Let's dissect this carefully.

3. **CHANGE AS OPPORTUNITY**

Every twist in the professional path, every unexpected change, can be reframed as an opportunity when approached with the right mindset and tools. In this chapter, we'll introduce you to a series of prompts designed specifically for job seekers navigating the complex and often uncertain waters of career transition. These prompts have been crafted to encourage reflection, strategic thinking, and proactive action. They will guide you in identifying hidden opportunities for professional growth.

By engaging with these prompts, job seekers will be empowered to transform challenges into growth opportunities, harnessing the potential that every change offers. Remember, it's not just about finding a new job; it's about leveraging the journey to become a stronger, more versatile professional.

PROMPT No 15

Goal

To highlight potential opportunities for your professional development that can be encountered throughout the job search process.

Prompt

Taking the position of a **career development advisor** specializing in **complex and high stake decision-making environments**, identify some **potential opportunities** for **professional growth** that might emerge during the **job-seeking journey**. Advise how I could recognize each of those opportunities. Include uncommon advice and underrated resources. Write using a **hopeful** tone and **engaging** writing style. Let's go through this systematically.

Taking the position of a **[profession]** specializing in the **[industry/topic]**, identify some **[opportunities/action plans]** for **[benefit/outcome]** that might emerge during the **[phase/process]**. Advise how I could recognize each of those **[opportunities/action plans]**. Include uncommon advice and underrated resources. Write using a **[tone]** and **[style]** writing style. Let's go through this systematically.

1. Assuming the role of a talent development consultant specializing in the healthcare sector, pinpoint potential avenues for skill enhancement that could surface during my transition to a new job. Provide guidance on how I can identify and seize these opportunities. Include unique suggestions and overlooked resources. Adopt an optimistic tone and compelling writing style. Let's dissect this systematically.
2. Acting as a professional growth mentor with a focus on the technology industry, highlight possible chances for personal advancement that may present themselves throughout my career change process. Advise on ways I can spot and grasp these opportunities. Incorporate unusual recommendations and less commonly known tools. Maintain an encouraging tone and captivating writing style. Let's tackle this in a stepwise manner.

PROMPT No. 16

To explore further the development of your skills for professional development.

Act like a **professional coach** who has a passion for **professional development**. Provide me with step-by-step **tactics** to **enhance my networking skills**. Share distinctive guidance and unexplored options. Write using a **confident** tone and a **conversational** writing style. Let's take this one step at a time.

Act like a **[profession]** who has a passion for **[area/topic]**. Provide me with a step-by-step **[tactics/best practices]** to **[benefit/outcome]**. Share distinctive guidance and unexplored options. Write using a **[tone]** and **[style]** writing style. Let's dissect this carefully.

1. Act like a public speaking coach who has a passion for helping immigrants improve their English accent. Provide me with a step-by-step plan to improve my public speaking skills. Give atypical suggestions and unsung resources. Write using a positive tone and assertive writing style. We should delve into this bit by bit.
2. Act like a speechwriter who has a passion for inspiring others. Provide me with a step-by-step strategy to enhance my written communication skills. Include uncommon advice and underrated

resources. Write using a hopeful tone and constructive writing style. Let's approach this gradually.

PROMPT No 17

Goal

To provide actionable strategies to fast-track your job search following a layoff, facilitating a quicker transition to a new job.

Prompt

Recently, I faced a **layoff** from my role as **a consultant** at **XYZ Inc**. I urgently need to **secure a new job**. Acting as a **job search strategist** with expertise in the **music industry**, brainstorm 3 **solutions** to my problem. Include uncommon advice and underrated resources.Write using a **motivated** tone and **reflective** writing style. Present a detailed and broad-ranging review

Formula

Recently, I faced a **[issue/challenge]** from my role as **[job/role]** at **[company name]**. I urgently need to **[benefit/outcome]**. Acting as a **[profession]** with expertise in the **[industry/topic]**, brainstorm **[number] [strategies/solutions]** to my problem. Include uncommon advice and underrated resources. Write using an **[tone]** and **[style]** writing style. Present a detailed and broad-ranging review.

Examples

1. Recently, I faced a layoff from my role as a software engineer at High Tech Inc. I'm in an urgent need to find new employment. Acting as a career transition coach with expertise in the tech sector, brainstorm 3 solutions to my problem. Express unusual guidance and neglected opportunities. Write using a hopeful tone and instructive writing style. Deliver a complete and meticulous response.
2. Recently, I was let go from my role as a marketing manager at ABC Inc. I'm in an urgent need to find new employment. Acting as a job market researcher with expertise in the consumer goods industry, brainstorm 5 solutions to my problem. Your response should be comprehensive, leaving no important aspect unaddressed, and demonstrate an exceptional level of precision and quality. Write using an empathetic tone and conversational writing style. Offer a meticulous and expansive response.

PROMPT No 18 [Follow-up to PROMPT No 17]

Goal

To help you understand the relative effectiveness of different job search strategies and prioritize your actions according to the most impactful approach.

Prompt

I want you to act as a **job search strategist** who specializes in **unemployable professionals**. Appraise the **solutions** suggested previously and rank them in order of **potential effectiveness**. Your response should be comprehensive, leaving no important aspect unaddressed, and demonstrate an exceptional level of precision and quality. Write using a **concise** tone and **assertive** writing style.

Formula

I want you to act as a **[profession]** who specializes in **[topic/industry]**. Appraise the **[strategies/solutions]** suggested previously and rank them in order of **[effectiveness/ likelihood of success]**. Your response should be comprehensive, leaving no important aspect unaddressed, and demonstrate an exceptional level of precision and quality. Write using a **[type]** tone and **[style]** writing style.

1. I want you to act as a career consultant. Appraise the three strategies suggested previously and rank them in order of their likelihood of success. Please provide a comprehensive explanation with detailed actions to follow. Write using a hopeful tone and conversational writing style.
2. I want you to act as an executive search consultant. Appraise the five solutions suggested previously and rank them in order of their potential effectiveness. Give a comprehensive and detailed breakdown. Write using an instructive tone and critical writing style.

PROMPT No 19

To offer valuable strategies that facilitate the acceptance and positive outlook towards your new beginnings and opportunities.

Performing as a **career transition coach**, could you propose some **insightful strategies** to aid in **embracing fresh starts and new opportunities** in preparation for my job search? Ensure that your response is thorough, precise, and of the highest quality possible. Write using a **motivated** tone and **creative** writing style. Let's address this point by point.

Performing as a **[profession],** could you propose some **[attribute/quality]** **[strategies/opportunities]** to aid in **[objective/outcome]** in preparation for my job search? Ensure that your response is thorough, precise, and of the highest quality possible. Write using a **[tone]** and **[style]** writing style. Let's address this point by point.

1. Performing as a life coach, could you propose some practical strategies to aid in looking at negative situations through positive lenses in preparation for my job search? Give a comprehensive and detailed breakdown. Write using an empathetic tone and reflective writing style. We should break this down into smaller parts.
2. Performing as an executive search consultant, could you propose some practical strategies to aid in getting into the right mindset in preparation for my job search? Please provide a comprehensive explanation with detailed actions to follow. Write using an instructive tone and persuasive writing style. Let's approach this gradually.

PROMPT No 20

To offer uplifting strategies to help you effectively deal with and overcome objections during your job search.

Act like a **motivational speaker** who specializes in **rejection**. Could you share some inspirational **approaches** to **handle and bounce back from rejections** in the **job-seeking process**? Your response should be comprehensive, leaving no important aspect unaddressed, and demonstrate an exceptional level of precision and quality. Write using an **empathetic** tone and **analytical** writing style. Let's dissect this carefully.

Formula

Act like a **[profession]** who specializes in **[area/topic]**. Could you share some **[attribute/descriptor]** **[approaches/insights]** to **[benefit/outcome]** in the **[process]**? Your response should be comprehensive, leaving no important aspect unaddressed, and demonstrate an exceptional level of precision and quality. Write using an **[tone]** and **[style]** writing style. Let's dissect this carefully.

Examples

1. As a resilience trainer focused on self-esteem, can you provide some empowering techniques to tackle and surmount disappointments during the job-hunting process? Your guidance should be all-encompassing, not overlooking any crucial detail, and should reflect the highest degree of accuracy and substance. Write using a supportive tone and systematic writing style. Let's break this down methodically.

2. Taking on the role of a career counselor with expertise in overcoming obstacles, could you divulge some encouraging strategies to deal with and rise above setbacks during the employment pursuit? Ensure your response is thorough, covering all pertinent points, and demonstrates an extraordinary standard of clarity and depth. Write using a compassionate tone and logical writing style. Let's examine this meticulously.

4. YOUR JOB SEARCH SUCCESS

Navigating your job search is as much about showcasing your past achievements as it is about planning your future steps. Here, you'll find prompts designed to sharpen your time management and storytelling skills, ensuring you present yourself as a standout candidate. The guidance offered is practical, aimed at helping you articulate your experiences compellingly and strategize effectively to land not just any job, but the right one for you.

Take these strategies to heart, using them to weave your professional experiences into engaging narratives, and to strategically approach your industry's job market. With an inspired and assertive approach, this chapter is set to boost your confidence, helping you to not only meet your career objectives but to exceed them.

PROMPT No 21

Goal

To provide guidance on how to effectively manage your time and tasks during the job search process, while maintaining a balanced lifestyle.

Prompt

Act as a **time management coach** specializing in the **technology industry**. What strategies can I implement to **manage my time and tasks effectively** during **my job-seeking journey**, while ensuring a **balanced lifestyle**? Share distinctive guidance and unexplored options. Write using a **motivated** tone and **assertive** writing style. Let's dissect this carefully.

Formula

Act as a **[profession]** specializing in the **[industry]**. What strategies can I implement to **[outcome]** during my **[process/journey]**, while ensuring a **[state/condition]**? Share distinctive guidance and unexplored options. Write using a **[type]** tone and **[style]** writing style. Let's dissect this carefully

Examples

1. Act as a productivity consultant specializing in the education sector. What strategies can I implement to manage my workload effectively during my career transition, while ensuring a stress-free environment? Suggest rare insights and underappreciated resources. Write using an authoritative tone and constructive writing style. Let's address this point by point.
2. Act as a time management coach specializing in the finance industry. What strategies can I implement to balance my job-seeking activities and personal life effectively, while ensuring a healthy lifestyle? Offer unconventional tips and lesser-known options. Write using a professional tone and constructive writing style. Let's go through this systematically.

PROMPT No 22

Goal

To aid in generating strong and persuasive stories based on the information and accomplishments presented in your resume.

Prompt

Could you assist in developing **ten compelling narratives** derived from **the experiences and achievements** as a **professional** listed on my resume? Present a detailed and broad-ranging response. Write using a **motivated** tone and **informative** writing style. We should delve into this bit by bit. Here is my resume: [**Insert resume**].

Could you assist in developing [**number**] [**descriptive quality**] [**narratives/stories**] derived from [**specific source or basis**] as a [**profession/position**] listed on my resume? Present a detailed and broad-ranging response. Write using a [**type**] tone and [**style**] writing style. We should delve into this bit by bit. Here is my resume: [**Insert resume**].

1. Could you assist in developing five inspiring narratives derived from my leadership roles as an account manager as listed on my resume? Propose a comprehensive and elaborate depiction. Write using an empathetic tone and critical writing style. Let's go through this systematically. Here is my resume: [Insert resume].
2. Could you assist in developing seven impactful stories derived from my career progression as a marketing executive listed on my resume? Propose a comprehensive and inspiration response. Write using an inspirational tone and engaging writing style. We should delve into this bit by bit. Here is my resume: [Insert resume].

PROMPT No 23

To provide a structured approach to effectively communicate powerful stories from your professional experiences during interviews or career discussions.

Could you guide me in **structuring my response** when asked to **share a powerful story from my professional experiences** for **maximum impact**? Offer unconventional strategies and underused approaches. Write using a **confident** tone and **conversational** writing style. Let's analyze this piece by piece.

Could you guide me on [**action**] when asked to [**question context**] for [**desired outcome**]? Offer unconventional strategies and underused approaches. Write using a [**type**] tone and [**style**] writing style. Let's analyze this piece by piece.

1. Could you guide me in framing my answer when asked about my greatest professional achievement for maximum impact? Please provide a comprehensive explanation with detailed actions to follow. Write using an instructive tone and critical writing style. Let's go through this systematically.
2. Could you guide me on presenting my response when asked about a challenging situation I overcame at work for maximum resonance? Ensure that your response is thorough, precise, and of the highest quality possible. Write using an empathetic tone and reflective writing style. We should delve into this bit by bit.

PROMPT No 24

To illustrate the application of the STAR [Situation, Task, Action, and Result] method in creating impactful professional narratives showing progress and success

Prompt

Could you present an example of a **business narrative** for an **engineer** in the **logistic industry**, using the STAR [Situation, Task, Action, and Result] method? Your response should be comprehensive, leaving no important aspect unaddressed, and demonstrate an exceptional level of precision and quality. Write using an **empathetic** tone and **constructive** writing style. Provide your response based on my resume. Let's unpack this topic. Here is my resume: **[Insert resume]**

Formula

Could you present an example of **[business narrative]** for a **[profession]** in the **[industry]**, using the STAR **[Situation, Task, Action, and Result]** method? Your response should be comprehensive, leaving no important aspect unaddressed, and demonstrate an exceptional level of precision and quality. Write using a **[type]** tone and **[style]** writing style. Provide your response based on my resume. Let's unpack this topic. Here is my resume: **[Insert resume]**

Examples

1. Can you provide an example of a transformational narrative for a project manager in the tech industry using the STAR [Situation, Task, Action, and Result] method? Your response should cover all important angles, deliver in-depth detail, and demonstrate superior quality. Write using a confident tone and an analytical writing style. Provide your response based on my resume. Let's break this down carefully. Here is my resume: [Insert resume]
2. Would you be able to deliver an example of a career progression narrative for a nurse in the healthcare industry utilizing the STAR [Situation, Task, Action, and Result] method? Please ensure that your response is exhaustive, goes into the necessary specifics, and showcases an unparalleled level of precision and substance. Write using a supportive tone and an authoritative writing style. Provide your response based on my resume. Let's dissect this systematically. Here is my resume: [Insert resume]

PROMPT No 25

To help identify critical considerations when hunting for the perfect job within your specialized domain, helping you align your search with career objectives.

Prompt

What essential questions should I explore when **seeking the ideal role** of **manager** within my specialized field of **technology**? Please provide a comprehensive explanation with detailed actions to follow. Write using a **hopeful** tone and **assertive** writing style. Let's go through this systematically.

Formula

What essential questions should I explore when **[phase/process]** of **[role/profession]** within my specialized field of **[field/sector]**? Please provide a comprehensive explanation with detailed actions to follow. Write using a **[type]** tone and **[style]** writing style. Let's go through this systematically.

1. As an expert in executive search within the medical sector, can you guide me on the vital inquiries I should make when pursuing the ideal Director role within the specialized field of Biotechnology? Offer an all-inclusive discourse with step-by-step guidance to follow. Write with an optimistic tone and decisive writing style. Let's break this down systematically.
2. As a senior career consultant with a focus on the finance industry, what critical questions should I delve into when looking for the ideal position as a Portfolio Manager within my specialized field of Investment Banking? Supply a thorough elucidation with explicit instructions to follow. Write using an encouraging tone and authoritative writing style. Let's dissect this in an orderly manner.

PROMPT No 26

Goal

To propose critical questions that will aid in the thoughtful and strategic pursuit of your ideal role within a specific field or industry.

Prompt

As a **seasoned career counselor** who specializes in the **manufacturing sector**, what **pivotal** inquiries should I consider while seeking the perfect role as a **production manager** within my **finance industry**? Please provide an exhaustive **discussion** with detailed **steps** to follow. Use an **inspiring** tone and **assertive** writing style. Let's dissect this carefully.

Formula

As a **[profession]** who specializes in the **[industry]**, what **[crucial/important]** inquiries should I consider while seeking the perfect role as a **[position]** within my **[industry/field]**? Please provide an exhaustive **[discussion/explanation]** with detailed **[steps/actions]** to follow. Write using a **[type]** tone and **[style]** writing style. Let's dissect this carefully.

Examples

1. Assuming the role of a career strategist with a strong emphasis on the healthcare sector, can you suggest some vital considerations I need to make when looking for the ideal position as a Healthcare Manager within my field of expertise? Please supply an exhaustive analysis with specific actions I should undertake. Adopt an encouraging tone and proactive writing style. Let's take this one step at a time.
2. As an experienced job search coach specializing in the healthcare sector, could you shed light on what essential considerations I should be making while on the lookout for the right role as a healthcare administrator within my area of specialization? Please furnish a comprehensive discourse with actionable steps to adhere to. Write using an encouraging tone and confident writing style. Let's break this down systematically.

5. SELF-DISCOVERY AND IMPROVEMENT

Embarking on a path of self-discovery and improvement is a powerful step towards not only securing the right job but also ensuring it aligns with who you are and who you aim to become. This chapter opens up avenues for introspection and growth, urging you to tap into your potential and polish your professional persona. The prompts guide you to extract the essence of your experiences, transform perceived weaknesses into strengths, and sharpen skills that resonate with your career ambitions.

We venture into the practice of framing your narrative, identifying transferable skills, and reinforcing your personal brand. From recognizing the gems in your resume to tailoring a 30-day skill enhancement plan, each step is an opportunity to evolve. These practices don't just prepare you for the job market; they shape you into a candidate of choice. With optimism and motivation as your backdrop, this chapter is your ally in converting every aspect of your professional journey into a beacon that guides you to your next destination.

PROMPT No 27

Goal

To provide actionable guidance on beginning a transformative journey for your professional self-discovery and personal growth.

Prompt

You are a **life coach** specializing in the field of **medicine**. Could you suggest **first** steps to embark on a **transformative journey for professional self-discovery**? Give exceptional advice and uncharted paths. Write in a **motivational** tone and **assertive** writing style. Let's dissect this carefully. Formulate your response based on the information in my LinkedIn profile: **[insert LinkedIn profile]**

Formula

You are a **[profession]** specializing in the field of **[industry/topic]**. Could you suggest **[descriptive quality]** steps to embark on a **[specific process]**? Give exceptional advice and uncharted paths. Write in a **[type]** tone and **[style]** writing style. Let's dissect this carefully. Formulate your response based on the information in my **[document/info]: [insert document/info]**

Examples

1. As a career coach with expertise in the technology sector, offer initial steps on how I should start my journey towards professional self-discovery. Provide unique advice and under-explored strategies. Write using an encouraging tone and authoritative writing style. Let's go through this systematically. Respond based on my provided career profile: [insert resume]
2. As a career strategist focusing on the education sector, please provide foundational steps I can take on a transformative journey for my professional self-discovery. Offer unique guidance and overlooked strategies. Write using an optimistic tone and clear writing style. Let's dissect this systematically. Develop your response based on the details in my professional portfolio: [insert professional portfolio]

PROMPT No 28 [Follow-up to PROMPT No 27]

Goal

To gain a clear understanding of your unique abilities and competencies and to identify areas for growth and development, based on the specific steps provided by ChatGPT for the previous prompt.

Provide me with **specifics** to **explore** the step of **assessing and improving my strengths and skills** provided by ChatGPT in response to the previous prompt. Suggest offbeat approaches and hidden gems. Write using a **motivated** tone and **constructive** writing style. Let's think about this step by step.

Provide me with **[specifics/best practices/insights]** to **[active verb]** the step of [select one step provided by ChatGPT in response to the previous prompt. Suggest offbeat approaches and hidden gems. Write using a **[tone]** and **[style]** writing style. Let's think about this step by step.

1. Provide me with best practices to explore the step of exploring my interests and curiosities. Share distinctive guidance and unexplored options. Write using a hopeful tone and conversational writing style. Let's think about this step by step.
2. Provide me with insights to expand on the step of setting clear goals. Write using an inspirational tone and assertive writing style.
Let's think about this step by step.

PROMPT No 29

To provide assistance in recognizing and articulating transferable skills that are apparent from the information presented in your resume.

In the role of a **career development consultant** with an emphasis on the **healthcare industry**, analyze my **resume** and highlight the **transferable skills** which could be beneficial in other areas. Provide unique insights and underrated resources. Write using an **optimistic** tone and **clear** writing style. Let's approach this step-by-step. Here is my resume: [insert resume]

In the role of a **[profession]** with an emphasis on the **[industry]**, analyze my **[document]** and highlight the **[specific skills/qualities]** which could be beneficial in other areas. Provide unique insights and underrated resources. Write using a **[type]** tone and **[style]** writing style. Let's approach this step-by-step. Here is my resume: **[insert resume]**

1. Acting as a career consultant with a specialty in the education sector, could you take a look at my resume and identify transferable skills that could potentially be applied in a different field? Offer atypical strategies and lesser-known resources for leveraging these skills. Write using a supportive tone and detailed writing style. Let's dissect this carefully. Here is my resume: [insert resume]
2. You are a career transition coach with a focus on the health sector. Could you review my resume and help identify transferable skills that could be beneficial in a new industry? Suggest novel

strategies and overlooked resources to highlight these skills. Write using an encouraging tone and instructive writing style. Let's tackle this systematically. Here is my resume: [insert resume]

PROMPT No 30

Goal

To provide help in identifying and appreciating personal strengths that are demonstrated through the experiences and achievements listed in your resume.

Prompt

As a **career strategist** with a focus on the **finance sector**, could you assist me in recognizing my **personal strengths** that are reflected through my past **experiences and accomplishments** listed on my resume? Suggest **innovative** ways and overlooked methods to present these **strengths**. Write in an **empowering** tone and **instructive** writing style. Let's take this one step at a time. Here is my resume: [insert resume]

Formula

As a **[profession]** with a focus on the **[industry],** could you assist me in recognizing my **[qualities/attributes]** that are reflected through my past **[achievements/experiences]** listed on my **[document]**? Suggest [innovative/unique] ways and overlooked methods to present these **[qualities/attributes]**. Write using a **[type]** tone and **[style]** writing style. Let's take this one step at a time. Here is my **[document]: [insert document]**

Examples

1. Acting as a personal development coach with expertise in the information technology industry, can you help me understand the strengths evident in my career history and achievements as laid out in my resume? Offer creative strategies and underutilized techniques to amplify these strengths. Write using a confident tone and clear writing style. Let's dissect this carefully. Here is my resume: [insert resume]
2. You're a career counselor specializing in the arts and design sector. Can you help me identify personal strengths demonstrated in the experiences and accomplishments on my resume? Provide inventive strategies and underappreciated tools to emphasize these strengths. Write using an encouraging tone and directive writing style. Let's go through this systematically. Here is my resume: [insert resume]

PROMPT No 31

Goal

To bring attention to your skills that can be effectively transferred and utilized in a new job role or environment.

Prompt

Acting as a **job market expert** who specializes in the **insurance industry**, can you help me bring out the **transferable skills** from my experiences and accomplishments listed in my **resume**? Provide **inventive** solutions and underutilized resources. Write using a **confident** tone and **clear** writing style. Let's approach this gradually. Here is my **resume: [insert resume]**

Formula

Acting as a **[profession]** who specializes in the **[industry]**, can you help me bring out the **[qualities/attributes]** from my **[experiences/achievements]** listed in my **[document]**? Provide **[innovative/unique]** solutions and underutilized resources. Write using a **[type]** tone and **[style]** writing style. Let's approach this gradually. Here is my **[document]: [insert document]**

1. As a professional development coach with a focus on the tech sector, can you assist me in identifying transferable skills evident in my work history and accomplishments as mentioned in my CV? Suggest rare methods and underappreciated techniques. Write using a hopeful tone and instructional writing style. Let's address this point by point. Here is my CV: [insert CV]

2. Act as a career consultant who specializes in skills transferability, could you help me highlight my transferable skills from the information given in my resume? Provide inventive and overlooked strategies. Write in an empowering tone and clear writing style. Let's dissect this carefully. Here is my resume: [insert resume]

PROMPT No 32

Goal

To provide valuable strategies for self-assessment, enabling the identification and understanding of your professional weaknesses for further improvement.

Prompt

As a **career coach** specializing in **personal growth**, can you share some **practical** strategies for self-assessment that would allow me to identify and improve upon my **professional weaknesses of lack of emotional empathy**? Offer distinctive advice and lesser-known techniques. Write using an **empathetic** tone and **instructive** writing style. Let's approach this gradually.

Formula

As a **[profession]** specializing in **[topic]**, can you share some **[descriptive adjective]** strategies for self-assessment that would allow me to identify and improve upon my **[aspect to be improved]**? Offer distinctive advice and lesser-known techniques. Write using a **[type]** tone and **[style]** writing style. Let's approach this gradually.

Examples

1. Acting as a personal development specialist with a focus on the tech sector, could you provide some effective self-assessment strategies that would help me recognize and work on my professional shortcomings of lack of communication skills? Suggest unique methods and overlooked resources. Write using an uplifting tone and clear writing style. Let's address this point by point.

2. As a professional development coach who specializes in self-improvement, can you suggest helpful self-assessment methods that can help me detect and develop my professional weaknesses of being impatient? Give creative suggestions and underestimated techniques. Write using a hopeful tone and motivational writing style. Let's dissect this carefully.

PROMPT No 33

To provide valuable practices that enable the conversion of perceived weaknesses into opportunities for your growth and professional development.

Prompt

As a **professional development coach** who specializes in **resilience**, can you provide valuable practices that can help me turn my perceived weakness in **decision-making** into **opportunities for career progression**? Offer novel tips and underestimated techniques. Write using a **hopeful** tone and **motivational** writing style. Let's dissect this carefully.

Formula

As a [profession] who specializes in [topic], can you provide valuable practices that can help me turn my perceived weakness in [specific weakness] into [desired outcome]? Offer novel tips and underestimated techniques. Write using a [type] tone and [style] writing style. Let's dissect this carefully.

Examples

1. Acting as a growth mentor with a focus on professional development, can you suggest effective ways to transform my perceived weakness in public speaking into stepping stones for my career growth? Provide innovative suggestions and underutilized resources. Write using an empathetic tone and instructive writing style. Let's address this point by point.
2. As a career advisor who specializes in transformational development, could you share some beneficial practices to convert my perceived weakness in time management into growth opportunities for professional development? Provide unorthodox tips and rarely exploited resources. Write using a motivated tone and assertive writing style. Let's take this one step at a time.

PROMPT No 34

Goal

To distill and share the most crucial portion of knowledge from a selected topic, aiming to provide you with a substantial understanding with minimal but focused learning.

Prompt

You are a **career coach**, and I want to understand the most essential aspects of **networking for job hunting** in **today's market**. Please distill the key principles and best practices in a concise summary, enabling me to **leverage networking effectively in my job search**. Write using a **positive** tone and **engaging** writing style. Let's dissect this carefully.

Formula

You are a [profession], and I want to understand the most essential aspects of [selected topic] in [context]. Please distill the key principles and best practices in a concise summary, enabling me to [specific goal related to the selected topic]. Write using a [type] tone and [style] writing style. Let's dissect this carefully.

Examples

1. You are an HR expert, and I need to quickly grasp the core elements of creating an appealing LinkedIn profile for job applications. Can you provide a brief guide highlighting the crucial components that will help me stand out to recruiters? Write using a professional tone and technical writing style. Let's address this point by point.
2. You are a professional resume writer, and I'm keen on understanding the fundamental principles of writing an effective cover letter tailored to a specific industry. Could you share a brief yet insightful overview that encapsulates the key factors and techniques I should consider? Write using a concise tone and descriptive writing style. Let's approach this gradually.

PROMPT No 35

Goal

To craft a comprehensive and beginner-friendly learning plan aimed at developing and improving your desired skills over a 30-day period.

Prompt

Act like a **professional coach** who has a passion for **professional development**. I'm seeking to enhance my **data analysis skills** for an upcoming job role. Can you create a beginner-friendly 30-day learning plan that systematically breaks down the key topics, includes a mix of **online resources, training workshops and books**, and ensures gradual progress?. Provide unusual recommendations and overlooked tools.

Formula

Act like a **[profession]** who has a passion for **[area/topic]**. I'm seeking to enhance my **[specific skill]** for **[contex]**. Can you create a beginner-friendly 30-day learning plan that systematically breaks down the key topics, includes a mix of **[learning methods or platforms]**, and ensures gradual progress?. Provide unusual recommendations and overlooked tools.

Examples

1. Act like a career consultant who has a passion for professional development. I want to develop my leadership abilities for a managerial position. Could you craft a 30-day step-by-step learning guide suitable for a beginner that incorporates readings, webinars, and practical exercises, aligning with my professional objectives?. Offer unconventional tips and lesser-known options.
2. Act like a job market researcher who has a passion for professional development. I'm interested in learning project management techniques for a new role I'm considering. Please outline a 30-day beginner-focused learning roadmap that includes a blend of tutorials, mentorship sessions, and self-assessment tools, helping me gauge my progress. Share unexpected advice and hidden gems.

PROMPT No 36

Goal

To actively assess and enhance your understanding of a chosen topic by challenging your knowledge with questions.

Prompt

I'm currently studying **market research** to apply for a **real estate research position**. Could you **challenge my understanding** with a series of **questions**? Ask me 10 questions. Write using a **professional** tone and **instructive** writing style.

I'm currently studying **[subject/topic]** to apply for a **[position]**. Could you **[objective/outcome]** my **[attribute/descriptor]** with a series of **[object]**? Ask me 10 questions. Write using an **[tone]** and **[style]** writing style.

1. I'm currently studying computer science. Could you challenge my understanding with a series of technical questions? Ask me 10 questions. Write using a professional tone and analytical writing style.
2. I'm currently studying marketing strategies to apply for a digital marketing position. Could you test my knowledge with a series of strategic questions? Ask me 10 questions. Write using a concise tone and assertive writing style.

PROMPT No 37 [Follow-up to PROMPT No 36]

To facilitate reflective learning by assessing the quality of your responses, pinpointing gaps or inaccuracies, and suggesting improved answers.

Could you **evaluate** the **strength** of my response, identify any **deficiencies**, and offer **enhanced answers** to address these shortcomings? Write using a **positive** tone and **assertive** writing style. Let's analyze this piece by piece. My response to question number No 2 is: **[response]**.

Could you **[objective/outcome]** the **[attribute/descriptor]** of my response, identify any **[attribute]**, and offer **[objective/outcome]** to address these shortcomings? Write using a **[type]** tone and **[style]** writing style. Let's dissect this carefully. My response to question number **[No]** is: **[insert response]**.

1. Could you evaluate the accuracy of my response, identify any missing details, and provide a more comprehensive answer to address these gaps? Write using a confident tone and critical writing style. Let's go through this systematically. My response to question number 5 is: Python is primarily used in data analysis.
2. Could you assess the completeness of my response, identify any knowledge gaps, and offer a more detailed answer to address these shortcomings? Write using an inspirational tone and analytical writing style We should delve into this bit by bit. My response to question number 7 is: SEO helps in increasing website traffic.

PROMPT No 38

Goal

To simplify and explain a complex topic that might be relevant in a job interview in such a way that it is easily comprehensible to you.

Prompt

Could you break down **artificial intelligence** into **simple, digestible** terms that **a novice** could easily grasp? Report an all-embracing and detailed synopsis. Write using a **professional** tone and **assertive** writing style.

Formula

Could you break down **[subject/topic]** into **[descriptive quality]** terms that a **[specific audience]** could easily grasp? Supply a detailed and holistic insight. Write using an **[tone]** and **[style]** writing style.

Examples

1. Could you break down quantum computing into simple, digestible terms that a high school student could easily grasp? Report an all-embracing and detailed synopsis. Write using an instructive tone and conversational writing style.
2. Could you break down the concept of blockchain into straightforward, digestible terms that a business professional with no technical background could easily grasp? Expound a thorough and complete discussion. Write using a professional tone and creative writing style.

PROMPT No 39

Goal

To outline the potential benefits and drawbacks of a career transition between two industries, taking into account current trends in the business landscape.

Prompt

As a **career transition expert** specializing in the **healthcare** and **technology** sectors, could you analyze the potential benefits and challenges of moving from a **healthcare role** to a **technology-based role**? Please consider recent trends and developments in both industries. Write using a **balanced** tone and **clear** writing style. Let's take this one step at a time.

Formula

As a **[profession]** specializing in the **[industry 1]** and **[industry 2]**, could you analyze the potential benefits and challenges of moving from a **[industry 1 role]** to a **[industry 2 role]**? Please consider recent trends and developments in both industries. Write using a **[type]** tone and **[style]** writing style. Let's take this one step at a time.

Examples

1. As a career consultant with experience in the finance and education sectors, can you delineate the possible advantages and disadvantages of a career shift from finance to education? Make sure to take into account the latest industry trends. Write using a thoughtful tone and instructive writing style. Let's dissect this carefully.
2. As a career advisor with a background in both the non-profit and corporate sectors, could you provide a comprehensive analysis of the pros and cons of transitioning from a non-profit role to a

corporate one? Please reflect on the current market conditions in both fields. Write using an objective tone and analytical writing style. Let's break this down slowly.

6. RESEARCH AND GET ORGANIZED FOR THE JOB SEARCH

Embarking on a job search is not just about applying to openings but also about deeply understanding where you're headed. In this chapter, the prompts guide you through strategic methodologies for uncovering emerging industries and aligning them with your unique set of skills and interests. You'll learn how to dissect company cultures and unravel values, all of which are critical when targeting companies.

With a focus on systematic analysis and comprehensive insights, the advice here is delivered with empathy and precision, designed to empower your job search with a level of depth that goes beyond the surface, ensuring you're not just prepared but thoroughly informed for your professional journey ahead.

PROMPT No 40

Goal
To provide valuable insights into specific industries associated with a specific subject that display strong prospects for future growth, aiding you in making informed career decisions.
Prompt
As a **career coach** with deep knowledge in **sustainable energy**, could you provide valuable insights into the job market and future growth prospects within this industry? Please offer guidance to support my career decisions. Write using a **supportive** tone and **informative** writing style. Let's tackle this systematically.
Formula
As a **[profession]** with deep knowledge in **[subject/industry]**, could you provide valuable insights into the job market and future growth prospects within this industry? Please offer guidance to support my career decisions. Write using a **[type]** tone and **[style]** writing style. Let's tackle this systematically.
Examples
1. As an expert career consultant specializing in Artificial Intelligence, can you share industry-specific insights and future growth trends in this field to assist my career planning? Share distinctive guidance and unexplored options. Write using a forward-thinking tone and instructive writing style. Let's break this down gradually. 2. As a job search strategist with expertise in digital marketing, could you offer a comprehensive outlook on the job prospects and future growth potential within this sector? Your insights will help me in making informed career choices. Suggest rare insights and underappreciated resources. Write using a constructive tone and clear writing style. Let's go through this step by step.

PROMPT No 41

To provide you with guidance in identifying emerging and growing industries, sectors, and rewarding professions and in making informed career decisions, aligning with your career and skills.

Prompt

Act as a **career strategist** with a focus on **industry analysis and growth trends**. What **strategies and methodologies** can I implement to **identify emerging industries and sectors, as well as rewarding professions** that align with my skills and interests for my next career move? Provide comprehensive insights, including **data analysis and networking techniques**. Write using an **informative** tone and **exploratory** writing style. Let's analyze this systematically. Here is my resume: **[insert resume]**

Formula

Act as a **[profession]** with a focus on **[subject/topic]**. What **[strategies/methodologies]** can I implement to **[benefit/outcome]** that align with my skills and interests for my next career move? Provide comprehensive insights, including **[resources]**. Write using a **[type]** tone and **[style]** writing style.. Let's analyze this systematically. Here is my resume: **[insert resume]**

Examples

1. Act as a labor market expert with a focus on industry forecasting and career planning. What action plans and tactics can I adopt to pinpoint flourishing industries, sectors, and rewarding professions that may be suitable for my next professional endeavor? Provide separately traditional and nontraditional approaches. Write using a practical and engaging writing style. Let's approach this step-by-step. Here is my resume: [insert resume]

2. Act as an employment trend analyst with a focus on long-term career positioning and growth sectors. What research methodologies and innovative approaches can I utilize to uncover burgeoning industries and professions that promise potential for personal and professional growth in my next role? Suggest all-inclusive and extensive strategies, both well-known and unconventional. Write using a futuristic and analytical writing style. Let's think about this progressively.

Goal

To compile information about the companies you want to apply for employment, focusing on aspects like company culture, values, and recent news.

Prompt

As a **career coach** specializing in **organizational culture**, could you guide me through the process of gathering information about **Microsoft's culture, values, and recent updates**? Your advice would be pivotal for **my job applications**. Write using an **empathetic** tone and a **detailed** writing style. Deliver a complete and meticulous response. Let's address this systematically.

Formula

As a **[profession]** specializing in **[specialization]**, could you guide me through the process of gathering information about **[company]'s [aspect 1]**, **[aspect 2]**, and **[aspect 3]**? Your advice would be pivotal for my **[context]**. Write using a **[tone]** tone and **[style]** writing style. Deliver a complete and meticulous response. Let's address this systematically.

Examples

1. As a professional job search strategist, could you help me understand how to compile crucial information about the values, culture, and latest news of the companies I am interested in applying to? Write using a supportive tone and informative writing style. Supply a detailed and holistic response. Let's dissect this topic step by step.

2. As a job search expert with a focus on company analysis, can you provide guidance on how to efficiently gather and analyze information about the culture, values, and recent updates of potential employers? Write using a constructive tone and a clear writing style. Give a comprehensive and detailed. Let's break this down gradually.

7. BALANCING CURRENT JOB AND JOB SEARCH

In this chapter, you'll learn the delicate art of managing the present while planning for the future. The job search, while currently employed, requires a fine balance — it's about being fully engaged in your current role while discreetly navigating the waters toward your next career move. This chapter offers strategies to handle this dual focus.

With each prompt, you'll gain insights into creating an effective balance, managing time, and handling the stress that naturally accompanies the pursuit of new opportunities. You'll also find guidance on setting clear boundaries that help you stay present in your current role without compromising your job search. Rare and unique strategies will be revealed, enabling you to move forward confidently and respectfully. This chapter isn't just about finding a new job — it's about mastering the transition with grace and efficiency.

PROMPT No 43

Goal

To provide strategies for managing time effectively while juggling a job search and current employment.

Prompt

As a **career coach** with expertise in **time management**, could you share some effective strategies for **balancing my job search with my current employment**? Please provide a detailed explanation using an **encouraging** tone and an **instructive** writing style. Include **uncommon** advice and **underrated** insights. Let's break this down step by step.

Formula

As a [profession] with expertise in [specialization], could you share some effective strategies for [desired objective]? Please provide a detailed explanation using a [tone] tone and [style] writing style. Include uncommon advice and underrated insights. Let's break this down step by step.

Examples

1. As an expert in job search strategies who also understands the complexities of maintaining current employment, could you offer some practical tips on managing time efficiently? Write using an empathetic tone and a clear writing style. Provide unique insights and overlooked opportunities. Let's dissect this topic carefully.
2. As a professional career strategist, could you help me devise a time management plan that will allow me to effectively search for new job opportunities while maintaining my performance at my current job? Please provide comprehensive guidance using a supportive tone and an instructive writing style. Include uncommon advice and underrated insights. Let's address this systematically.

PROMPT No 44

Goal

To provide advice on maintaining performance at the current job while job searching.

Prompt

As a **professional career coach** specializing in **career transitions** for professionals in the **manufacturing industry**, what advice can you give me on **keeping up with my current job responsibilities while simultaneously searching for a new job**? Give a comprehensive answer with actionable steps, using a **motivating** tone and an **instructive** writing style. Let's go through this systematically.

Formula

As a [profession] specializing in [topic] for professionals in the [industry], what advice can you give me on [desired objective]? Give a comprehensive answer with actionable steps, using a [type] tone and [style] writing style. Let's go through this systematically.

Examples

1. Being an expert in career transitions, could you share insights on how to balance my performance at my current job while actively searching for a new opportunity? Please provide a detailed explanation, employing an empathetic tone and a clear writing style. Let's break this down step by step.

2. As a seasoned job search advisor for top executives in the tech industry, can you suggest strategies on how to effectively maintain my productivity at my present job while actively exploring new career opportunities? Present a thorough and extensive overview using an inspiring tone and a clear writing style. Let's take this one step at a time.

PROMPT No 45

Goal

To provide strategies for handling stress while managing a job search and current employment.

Prompt

Act as a **career consultant** specializing in **time management** for professionals in the **tech industry**, could you provide some unique strategies for **effectively balancing current job responsibilities with job search activities**? Write using a **motivational** tone and **assertive** writing style. Provide unique insights and overlooked opportunities. Let's address this point by point.

Formula

Act as a [profession] specializing in [topic] for professionals in the [industry], could you provide some unique strategies for [desired outcome]? Write using a [type] tone and [style] writing style. Provide unique insights and overlooked opportunities. Let's address this point by point.

Examples

1. Act as a job search expert specializing in stress management for professionals in the healthcare industry, could you provide some unique strategies for maintaining well-being during a job search while working full time? Write using a calming tone and empathetic writing style. Provide unique insights and overlooked opportunities. Let's address this point by point.

2. Act as a career coach specializing in career transition for professionals in the finance industry, could you provide some unique strategies for seamless transition between roles within the industry? Write using a supportive tone and clear writing style. Provide unique insights and overlooked opportunities. Let's address this point by point.

PROMPT No 46

To provide advice on setting boundaries between the current job and job search.

As a **career counselor** with expertise in **maintaining work-life balance**, can you provide **practical** strategies for **establishing boundaries** between my **current job** and **my job search activities**? Impart unconventional wisdom and under-the-radar insights. Let's tackle this with a **practical** tone and an **instructive** writing style.

As a **[profession]** with expertise in **[specific area]**, can you provide **[descriptive attribute]** strategies for **[specific task]** between my **[current situation]** and **[desired situation]**? Impart unconventional wisdom and under-the-radar insights. Let's tackle this with a **[type]** tone and a **[style]** writing style.

1. Given your background as a job search consultant focused on maintaining professional equilibrium, could you share useful techniques for separating my ongoing employment from my job search efforts? Provide unusual recommendations and overlooked techniques. Please adopt a thoughtful tone and a comprehensive writing style. Let's break this down in detail.
2. As a career coach specializing in juggling multiple professional responsibilities, could you offer insight into setting boundaries between my existing job and my job search process? Give atypical strategies and less recognized insights. Let's unravel this with a balanced tone and a systematic writing style.

PROMPT No 47

To provide strategies for maintaining motivation during a job search while employed.

As a **career coach** with a focus on **motivation and goal-setting**, could you share your strategies for **maintaining my drive** during a **job search** while **currently employed**? Please use a **motivational** tone and an **encouraging** writing style. Let's explore this step-by-step.

As a **[profession]** with a focus on **[specialization]**, could you share your strategies for **[desired outcome]** during a **[specific task]** while **[current situation]**? Please use a **[type]** tone and a **[style]** writing style. Let's explore this step-by-step.

1. Given your background as a career consultant specializing in motivation and perseverance, could you suggest effective methods to keep my enthusiasm alive during my job search despite being presently employed? Write with an inspirational tone and a supportive writing style. Let's take a thorough look at this.
2. As a job search advisor who prioritizes motivation and resilience, could you offer strategies on how to stay motivated during my job search while I am still working? Please use a positive tone and an empowering writing style. Let's break this down carefully.

PROMPT No 48

Goal

To provide advice on how to handle job interviews while currently employed.

Prompt

As a **job search expert** specializing in **time management** for **working professionals**, can you suggest some **innovative** strategies for **efficiently preparing for job interviews while managing current job responsibilities**? Provide your recommendations in a step-by-step manner, using a **motivational** tone and **clear** writing style. Let's dissect this systematically.

Formula

As a **[profession]** specializing in **[topic]** for **[target audience]**, can you suggest some **[descriptive adjective]** strategies for **[desired outcome]**? Provide your recommendations in a **[method of delivery]**, using a type **[tone]** and **[style]** writing style. Let's dissect this systematically.

Examples

1. Given your experience as a career coach focused on work-life balance, can you provide insights on how to effectively manage time and energy while preparing for job interviews amidst handling current job duties? Use an empathetic tone and instructive writing style. Let's take this one step at a time.
2. As a career consultant with a focus on time and stress management, can you share your top strategies for successfully juggling job interview preparations with current job obligations? Please use a calming tone and an instructive writing style. Let's approach this gradually.

PROMPT No 49

Goal

To provide strategies for dealing with feelings of guilt about job searching while employed.

Prompt

As a **career counselor** specializing in **job transition ethics** for the **real estate industry**, could you suggest some **empathetic** strategies to help me manage **feelings of guilt about job searching while still employed**? Use a **supportive** tone and a **clear** writing style. Let's break this down into manageable steps.

Formula

As a **[profession]** specializing in **[topic]** for the **[industry]**, could you suggest some **[descriptive adjective]** strategies to help me manage **[specific emotional challenge]**? Use a **[type]** tone and a **[style]** writing style. Let's break this down into manageable steps.

Examples

1. Given your expertise as a career coach focused on emotional well-being for the tech industry, can you share advice on dealing with the guilt associated with seeking a new job while currently employed? Please use a compassionate tone and a straightforward writing style. Let's dissect this systematically.
2. As a job search expert who understands the emotional complexity of job transitions for the health care sector, can you provide unique strategies for managing feelings of guilt when job searching

while still holding a job? Use an understanding tone and an encouraging writing style. Let's approach this gradually.

PROMPT No 50

Goal
To provide advice on how to keep a job search confidential while currently employed.

Prompt
As a **career coach** who specializes in **covert job searches**, can you provide me with **discreet** strategies to **maintain confidentiality** while **seeking new job opportunities during my current employment**? Present detailed and broad-ranging solutions. Let's delve into this with a **respectful** tone and a **strategic** writing style.

Formula
As a **[profession]** who specializes in **[specific area]**, can you provide me with **[descriptive attribute]** strategies to **[specific task]** while **[current situation]**? Present detailed and broad-ranging solutions. Let's delve into this with a **[type]** tone and a **[style]** writing style.

Examples
1. Given your background as a job search consultant with an emphasis on discretion, what are some key methods to uphold privacy while I'm searching for a new job during my current employment? Provide unique and overlooked solutions. Please use a sensitive tone and a detailed writing style. Let's address this step by step.
2. As a career advisor experienced in secret job searches, could you advise me on how to keep my job hunt confidential while I'm still employed? Provide unique and overlooked strategies. Write with a cautious tone and a comprehensive writing style. Let's unravel this meticulously.

PROMPT No 51

Goal
To provide strategies for staying focused on the current job while job searching.

Prompt
As a **career consultant** with expertise in **productivity**, could you provide strategies for **staying focused** on my current role while **actively seeking a new job with another company**? Share rare and lesser-known strategies. Please use a **clear** tone and a **direct** writing style. Let's dive into this step-by-step.

Formula
As a **[profession]** with expertise in **[specialization]**, could you provide strategies for **[desired outcome]** on my current role while **[specific situation]**? Share rare and lesser-known strategies. Please use a **[tone]** and a **[writing style]**. Let's dive into this step-by-step.

Examples
1. Given your background as a career coach focusing on multitasking and time management, could you share effective methods for maintaining my focus on my current job while I am searching for

a new one at another company? Provide unusual and overlooked methods. Write with an instructive tone and an engaging writing style. Let's examine this in detail.

2. As a professional development advisor with a concentration on focus and productivity, could you recommend techniques on how to stay committed to my current job while seeking a new one at a different company? Share rare and lesser-known techniques. Please use an assertive tone and a straightforward writing style. Let's break this down thoroughly.

PROMPT No 52

Goal
To provide advice on how to handle a job offer while currently employed.

Prompt
As an experienced **career counselor** with expertise in **negotiation and decision-making**, could you provide insights on how to **manage a job offer from another company while still employed**? Write using a **practical** tone and a **detailed** writing style. Let's dissect this systematically.

Formula
As an experienced [profession] with expertise in [specialization], could you provide insights on how to [desired outcome] while [specific situation]? Write using a [type] tone and [style] writing style. Let's dissect this systematically.

Examples

1. Given your background as a recruitment advisor with a focus on career transitions, could you share your knowledge on managing a job offer when I am already employed? Please write using an empathetic tone and a clear writing style. Let's delve into this step by step.

2. As a job transition coach with extensive experience, could you offer advice on how to handle a job offer from a different company while I am still employed? Write using a balanced tone and a precise writing style. Let's break this down into manageable parts.

8. ELEVATOR SPEECH/TELL ME ABOUT YOURSELF

In the fast-paced world of professional growth and job transitions, the ability to succinctly and persuasively convey one's achievements and aspirations can make all the difference. This chapter emphasizes the importance of crafting compelling narratives that not only highlight individual accomplishments but also align with specific job roles and industry requirements.

Here, we focus on refining your story to match the beats of your career's past highlights, present engagement, and future aspirations. We'll delve into tailoring your responses to encapsulate your achievements, competencies, and the value you bring, all within the framework of the specific role and company you're targeting. With step-by-step guidance, this chapter equips you to create an elevator pitch that is not just a narrative of your past but a vision of your potential future, setting you up for interview success.

PROMPT No 53 [3-Step Prompt]

Goal

To obtain a response to answer the question "Tell me about yourself", based on your resume and the job you are applying for

Step 1 - Go to ChatGPT to Obtain a breakdown of the job description

Prompt

You are a **seasoned hiring manager** specializing in the **tech industry**. You are responsible for this job posting. Highlight the **3** most important **responsibilities** in this job description: [insert job description]

Formula

You are a **[profession]** specializing in the **[industry]**. You are responsible for this job posting. Highlight the **[number]** most important **[responsibilities/skills]** in this job description: **[insert job description]**

Step 2 - Obtain a customized answer from ChatGPT based on your resume

Prompt

Based on the **3** most important **responsibilities**, help me structure an answer to the "Tell me about yourself" interview question based on my resume. Use the **Present, Past, and Future framework**. Start with the present [what I'm doing now], then talk about a few select work experiences I've done in the past, and end with the future [why I want to work in this new position] Keep the answer within 300 words. Here's my resume: **[insert resume]**

Formula

Based on the **[number]** most important **[responsibilities/skills],** help me structure an answer to the "Tell me about yourself" interview question based on my resume. Use the **[framework/approach]**. Start with the present [what I'm doing now], then talk about a few select work experiences I've done in the past, and end with the future [why I want to work in this new position] Keep the answer within 300 words. Here's my resume: **[insert resume]**

Step 3 - Further refine the "Future" section for the role you're applying for, if needed, with ChatGPT

The **"Future" section** is **too vague**. Based on the job description, please give me 1 specific example why working at the **ABC Company Inc.** would be a great fit for me based on my previous experiences. Include keywords from the job description where appropriate. Prioritize unorthodox, lesser known advice in your answer. Do not make information up. Here's the job description: **[insert job description]**

The **[section]** is **[attribute or descriptor]**. Based on the job description, please give me 1 specific example why working at **[company]** would be a great fit for me based on my previous experiences. Include keywords from the job description where appropriate. Prioritize unorthodox, lesser known advice in your answer. Do not make information up. Here's the job description: **[insert job description]**

PROMPT No 54

To highlight various competencies and successes across your career. By structuring them according to the situation, actions, and results, you can create compelling narratives that strengthen your resume and provide valuable examples to share during interviews.

Act as a **copywriter** specializing in the **tech industry**. I'm looking to draft a power story showcasing my success in **leading a software development project for a startup**. The context is a **tight deadline with limited resources**. Please guide me in constructing this story with a logical sequence of the background, actions, and measurable delivery success in a concise paragraph. Write using a **confident** tone and **persuasive** writing style. Here is my resume as a reference: **[insert resume]**

Act as a **[profession]** specializing in the **[industry]**. I'm looking to draft a power story showcasing my success in **[specific accomplishmen/skill]**. The context is [brief description of the situation or event]. Please guide me in constructing this story with a logical sequence of the background, actions, and measurable effects in a concise paragraph. Write using a **[type]** tone and **[style]** writing style. Here is my resume as a reference: **[insert resume]**

1. Act as a copywriter specializing in theeducation iindustry. I need to compose a power story that illustrates my ability to turn around a struggling school's academic performance. The scenario was enhancing teaching methods and student engagement. Can you help me articulate this story by detailing the situation, outlining the key actions, and summarizing the improved academic results in one paragraph? Write using a professional tone and persuasive writing style. Here is my resume as a reference: [insert resume]
2. Act as a copywriter specializing in the healthcare industry. I want to create a power story that reflects my innovative approach in implementing a patient care protocol in a hospital. The background involves addressing inefficiencies in the existing care pathway. Can you help me craft this story by describing the situation, actions taken, and the measurable improvement in

patient satisfaction in one paragraph? Write using a confident tone and technical writing style. Here is my resume as a reference: [insert resume]

PROMPT No 55

Goal

To succinctly convey a compelling career story that aligns with the requirements of a specific job role, focusing on key achievements and using strong, action-oriented language.

Prompt

Assume the role of a **career coach** specializing in **narrative crafting**. Produce a compelling career story that aligns with the requirements of a **project manager role**, highlighting my **key achievements**, and using strong, action-oriented language. Provide an all-encompassing career story. Write using a **motivational** tone and **clear** writing style. Here is my understanding of the position's requirements: **[insert job requirements/description]**. Here are my key achievements: **[insert achievements]**

Formula

Assume the role of a **[profession]** specializing in **[subject/topic]**. Produce a compelling career story that aligns with the requirements of a **[specific job role]**, highlighting my **[highlighting factor]**, and using strong, action-oriented language. Provide an all-encompassing career story. Write using a **[type]** tone and **[style]** writing style. Here is my understanding of the position's requirements: **[insert job requirements/description]**. Here are my key achievements: **[insert achievements]**

Examples

1. You're a job search consultant who has a knack for storytelling. Produce a powerful career narrative that aligns with the requirements of a business analyst role, focusing on major achievements and utilizing impactful, action-driven language. Share a comprehensive and detailed career narrative. Write with an encouraging tone and a professional writing style. Here is my understanding of the position's requirements: [insert job requirements/description]. Here are my key achievements: [insert achievements]
2. Act as a career narrative expert with experience in job hunting. Produce a persuasive career story in line with the needs of a software engineer role, accentuating pivotal accomplishments and making use of dynamic, action-packed language. Provide a comprehensive and extensive career story. Write using an inspiring tone and a confident writing style. Here is my understanding of the role's requirements: [insert job requirements/description]. Here are my key achievements: [insert achievements]

PROMPT No 56

Goal

To meticulously organize and articulate personal narratives showcasing key competencies, enhancing interview preparedness for a specific job role, and effectively conveying one's value to potential employers.

Prompt

Assume the role of a **personal branding strategist** with expertise in the **tech industry**. I am preparing for an interview for a **managerial position** at a **reputable software development**

company. I have a collection of experiences that showcase various competencies such as **leadership, cross-group collaboration, and influencing**. Guide me in meticulously organizing these stories by name, prioritizing them based on the job requirements, and identifying the key competency each narrative demonstrates. This will be a part of my interview preparation to ensure that I articulate my value proposition effectively to the potential employer. Here are the job requirements: **[insert job requirements]**. Here are the stories: **[insert stories]**.

Formula

Assume the role of a **[profession]** with expertise in the **[industry]**. I am preparing for an interview for a **[specific position]** at a [company description]. I have a collection of experiences that showcase various competencies such as **[list of competencies]**. Guide me in meticulously organizing these stories by name, prioritizing them based on the job requirements, and identifying the key competency each narrative demonstrates. This will be a part of my interview preparation to ensure that I articulate my value proposition effectively to the potential employer. Here are the job requirements: **[insert job requirements]**. Here are the stories: **[insert stories]**.

Examples

1. Assume the role of a narrative coach specializing in the healthcare sector. I am gearing up for an interview for a supervisory role at a leading hospital. I possess a repertoire of experiences illustrating competencies like patient advocacy, team coordination, and crisis management. Assist me in systematically organizing these stories by name, ranking them in alignment with the job prerequisites, and pinpointing the core competency each story embodies. This endeavor is crucial for my interview readiness, enabling me to convincingly convey my capability and fit to the hiring panel. Here are the job requirements: [insert job requirements]. Here are the stories: [insert stories].
2. Assume the role of a personal branding consultant with a focus on the finance industry. I am prepping for an interview for an executive position at a well-established investment firm. My journey encompasses a variety of situations reflecting competencies like strategic foresight, stakeholder engagement, and risk management. Aid me in diligently organizing these stories by name, prioritizing them contingent on the job specifications, and distinguishing the key competency each tale elucidates. This preparation is integral to my interview strategy, ensuring I present a compelling narrative of my qualifications to prospective employers. Here are the job requirements: [insert job requirements]. Here are the stories: [insert stories].

9. LINKEDIN PRESENCE

Creating a standout LinkedIn presence is crucial in today's job market. Your profile often serves as the first point of contact with potential employers and can make a lasting impression. This chapter is about constructing a LinkedIn profile that speaks volumes about your professional journey, showcasing your unique skills, experiences, and achievements in a way that resonates with your industry's community.

From penning a compelling 'About' section that tells your career story to formulating a headline that captures your essence in under 220 characters, this chapter guides you through each element of your profile. It will provide insights on optimizing your profile with strategic keywords and present techniques for enhancing profile visibility and engagement. You'll also learn how to translate your resume into a narrative that fits LinkedIn's format and tone, ensuring that your online persona is as dynamic and impactful as you are in person.

PROMPT No 57

Goal

To create a succinct and engaging 'About' section for your LinkedIn profile that accurately reflects your skills, experiences, and achievements as listed on your resume.

Prompt

As a **LinkedIn profile specialist** with expertise in **personal branding**, can you craft an engaging 'About' section that effectively captures my **skills, experiences, and achievements** as stated in my **resume**? Write using a creative tone and a step-by-step approach. Keep your response under 300 words. Let's tackle this bit by bit. Here is my resume: **[insert resume]**

Formula

As a **[profession]** with expertise in **[specialization]**, can you **[desired outcome]** that effectively captures my **[specific attributes]** as stated in my **[specific document]**? Write using a **[tone]** and **[approach]**. Keep your response under 300 words. Let's tackle this bit by bit. Here is my resume: **[insert resume]**

Examples

1. Considering your background as a career counselor specializing in online presence, could you guide me on developing a succinct 'About' section on LinkedIn that mirrors the skills, experiences, and accomplishments listed in my resume? Write using an encouraging tone and a detailed writing style. Keep your response under 300 words. Let's break this down systematically. Here is my resume: [insert resume]

2. As a digital branding expert with focus on professional networking platforms, could you help me create an impressive 'About' section for my LinkedIn profile that accurately reflects the skills, experiences, and achievements on my resume? Write using a motivational tone and a concise writing style. Keep your response under 300 words. Let's dissect this progressively. Here is my resume: [insert resume]

Goal

To create an engaging and professional LinkedIn headline that effectively reflects your skills, experiences, and achievements as listed on your resume, enhancing your online visibility and professional appeal.

Prompt

As a **LinkedIn profile specialist** with expertise in **personal branding**, can you produce **an engaging and professional LinkedIn headline** that effectively captures my **skills, experiences**, and **achievements** as stated in my resume? The LinkedIn headline should have 220 characters or less. Write using a **motivated** tone and **creative** writing style. Let's tackle this bit by bit. Here is my resume: [insert resume]

Formula

As a **[profession]** with expertise in **[specialization]**, can you produce a **[desired outcome]** that effectively captures my **[specific attributes]** as stated in my **[specific document]**? The LinkedIn headline should have 220 characters or less. Write using a **[type]** tone and **[style]** writing style. Let's tackle this bit by bit. Here is my resume: **[insert resume]**

Examples

1. Considering your background as a career counselor specializing in online presence, could you produce a succinct and professional LinkedIn headline that mirrors the skills, experiences, and accomplishments listed in my resume? The LinkedIn headline should have 220 characters or less. Write using an encouraging tone and a detailed writing style. Let's break this down systematically. Here is my resume: [insert resume]
2. As a digital branding expert with focus on professional networking platforms, could you produce an impressive and professional LinkedIn headline that accurately reflects the skills, experiences, and achievements on my resume? The LinkedIn headline should have 220 characters or less. Write using a motivational tone and a concise writing style. Let's dissect this progressively. Here is my resume: [insert resume]

PROMPT No 59

Goal

To create an engaging and professional LinkedIn headline that effectively incorporates given keywords, enhancing the individual's online visibility and professional appeal.

Prompt

As a **LinkedIn profile expert** who specializes in **keyword optimization**, could you craft for me **an engaging and professional LinkedIn headline** that incorporates the keywords **'Project Management'**, **'Leadership'**, and **'Strategic Planning'**? The LinkedIn headline should have 220 characters or less. Write using an **informative** tone and an **engaging** approach. Let's dissect this progressively.

Formula

As a **[profession]** who specializes in **[specialization]**, could you craft for me a **[desired outcome]** that incorporates the keywords **'[Keyword1]'**, **'[Keyword2]'**, and **'[Keyword3]'**? The LinkedIn headline should have 220 characters or less. Write using a **[type]** tone and **[style]** writing style. Let's dissect this progressively.

1. Considering your expertise as a personal branding consultant with a focus on LinkedIn profiles, can you craft for me an engaging and professional LinkedIn headline that effectively uses the keywords 'Data Analysis', 'Problem Solving', and 'Process Improvement'? The LinkedIn headline should have 220 characters or less. Write using an encouraging tone and a detailed style. Let's tackle this bit by bit.
2. As a career coach specialized in online branding, can you craft for me an engaging and professional LinkedIn headline that incorporates the keywords 'Product Development', 'Innovation', and 'Team Leadership'? The LinkedIn headline should have 220 characters or less. Write using a motivational tone and a concise writing style. Let's approach this systematically.

PROMPT No 60

Goal

To create a LinkedIn profile title that succinctly and accurately portrays your unique value proposition and area of specialty, enhancing your professional brand.

Prompt

Given your expertise as a **personal branding consultant** for professionals in the **manufacturing industry**, can you create **a succinct** LinkedIn profile title that effectively communicates my unique value proposition and emphasizes my specialty? Write using an **empathetic** tone and **clear** writing style. Let's dissect this systematically. My value proposition is leadership without authority and my area of specialty is technology.

Formula

Given your expertise as a **[profession]** for professionals in the **[industry]**, can you create a **[description]** LinkedIn profile title that seffectively communicates my unique value proposition and emphasizes my specialty? Write using a **[type]** tone and **[style]** writing style. Let's dissect this systematically. My value proposition is **[insert value proposition]** and my specialty is **[insert specialty/topic]**

1. As a LinkedIn branding expert for professionals in the corporate finance sector, could you create a concise LinkedIn profile title that accurately reflects my unique value proposition and showcases my area of specialty? Write in an instructive tone and detailed style. Let's tackle this step by step. My unique value proposition is 'Business Strategy' and specialty is 'Insurance'.
2. As a career coach specialized in online branding for professionals in the shipping industry, can you create a compact LinkedIn profile title that accurately conveys my unique value proposition and my area of specialty? Write using a supportive tone and a step-by-step writing style. Let's approach this progressively. My unique value proposition is 'Project Management' and my specialty is 'Logistics'.

PROMPT No 61

To pinpoint the essential LinkedIn keywords for your role, position, and industry, enhancing your LinkedIn profile's visibility and searchability.

As a **career advisor** with expertise in **LinkedIn optimization**, could you help me identify the most significant LinkedIn keywords for my role as a **'Data Scientist'**, and the **'Tech'** industry? Write using a **motivated** tone and **creative** writing style. Let's delve into this systematically.

As a **[profession]** with expertise in **[specialization]**, could you help me identify the most significant LinkedIn keywords for my role as a **[role/position]** and the **'[Industry]'** industry? Write using a **[type]** tone and **[style]** writing style. Let's delve into this systematically.

1. Given your proficiency as a LinkedIn branding specialist, can you guide me in pinpointing the essential LinkedIn keywords for my role as an 'HR Manager' and the 'Human Resources' sector? Write using an inspirational tone and creative writing style. Let's approach this step by step.
2. As a professional development coach focused on digital branding, can you assist me in determining the crucial LinkedIn keywords for my role as a 'Marketing Specialist' and the 'Marketing and Advertising' industry? Write using a motivated tone and technical writing style. Let's dissect this progressively.

PROMPT No 62

To compose a concise, compelling 'About' section for your LinkedIn profile using information from your resume, boosting your profile's appeal and readability.

Act as a **LinkedIn consultant** with a focus on the **job search**. Could you **craft an engaging 'About' section for my LinkedIn profile** using the information from my **resume**? Include strategies to **enhance the appeal and readability of my profile**. Provide an all-encompassing response, leaving no stone unturned. Ensure my 'About' section is of 2,600 characters or less. Write using an **encouraging** tone and **clear** writing style. Let's break this down bit by bit.

Act as a **[profession]** with a focus on **[topic/subject]**. Could you **[action/task]** using the information from my **[resource/document]**? Include strategies to **[benefit/outcome]**. Provide an all-encompassing response, leaving no stone unturned. Ensure my 'About' section is of 2,600 characters or less.Write using a **[type]** tone and **[style]** writing style. Let's break this down bit by bit.

1. Assume the role of a career coach specializing in personal branding. What are some effective techniques to convert my resume details into a concise yet compelling 'About' section on LinkedIn? Let's aim for improving the overall appeal and readability of my profile. Your response should be thorough, covering all necessary points. Ensure my 'About' section is of 2,600

characters or less.Write using a motivating tone and professional writing style. Let's take this one step at a time.
2. You are a personal branding expert with a knack for job searching. How can I transform my resume content into a succinct, attractive 'About' section on LinkedIn? What can I do to increase the visual appeal and readability of my profile? I'm looking for a comprehensive plan that covers all angles. Ensure my 'About' section is of 2,600 characters or less. Write using a positive tone and a straightforward writing style. Let's dissect this carefully.

PROMPT No 63

Goal
To develop a succinct, engaging LinkedIn post on a specified topic, formatted with bullet points and enhanced with relevant hashtags for greater visibility

Prompt
Assume the role of a **social media strategist** who is well-versed in **job search techniques**. How can I create a **succinct** and **engaging** LinkedIn post on the topic of '**The future of remote work**', using **a bullet point** format and enhanced with relevant hashtags fo**r improved visibility**? Provide a thorough and comprehensive response. Write using a **dynamic** tone and a **clear** writing style. Let's break this down step by step.

Formula
Assume the role of a **[profession]** who is well-versed in **[subject/topic]**. How can I create a **[characteristic 1]** and **[characteristic 2]** LinkedIn post on the topic of **[specified topic]**, using a **[format style]** and enhanced with relevant hashtags for **[desired outcome]**? Provide a **[level of depth]** response. Write using a **[type]** tone and **[style]** writing style.. Let's break this down step by step.

Examples
1. You're a content marketing expert who specializes in job search strategy. Could you guide me on composing a brief yet impactful LinkedIn post about 'The role of AI in job recruitment', formatted with bullet points and supplemented with relevant hashtags for maximum reach? Share your comprehensive and detailed response. Write with a confident tone and a conversational writing style. Let's take this one step at a time.
2. Act as a LinkedIn marketing consultant with expertise in job seeking. What are the best practices to craft a short, compelling LinkedIn post on 'Effective networking strategies', organized with bullet points and boosted with pertinent hashtags for better exposure? Provide a comprehensive and extensive response. Write using an inspiring tone and an assertive writing style. Let's dissect this carefully.

10. NETWORKING

Networking is the lifeline of career progression, and this chapter is your guide to doing it right. It's about crafting tailored messages that grab attention, asking insightful questions that show you've done your homework, and making connections that count. This chapter equips you with strategies to reach out effectively, ensuring you're not just another request in the inbox but a memorable interaction leading to fruitful professional relationships. From personalized messages to respectful requests for introductions, you'll learn the fine art of networking.

By following the structured prompts, you'll gain the skills to compose persuasive messages, frame engaging posts, and articulate your value in ways that are both respectful and effective. Whether you're seeking advice, requesting a resume referral, or simply looking to expand your professional network, the guidance in this chapter will help you navigate these interactions with tact, professionalism, and a touch of personal flair.

PROMPT No 64 [3-Step Prompt]

Goal
To connect through LinkedIn with someone you don't know, by personalizing your message and standing out from the crowd.

Step 1 - To obtain the LinkedIn profile of the person you want to connect with.

Action
Go to their LinkedIn profile > click on "More" > Save to PDF > open the PDF > CMD or CTRL + A to select everything, and CMD or CTRL + C to copy to your clipboard

Step 2 - Go to ChatGPT to generate a summary of the person's career and accomplishments.

Prompt
You are an experienced **career coach** with over 20 years of professional experience. Based on the following LinkedIn profile, could you please generate **a summary of this person's career and accomplishments and highlight their top three achievements**? List the 3 achievements under separate headers. Please provide as much detail as possible, including relevant experiences, skills, and accomplishments that showcase the person's expertise in their **[role/industry]**. Here is the LinkedIn profile: **[insert LinkedIn profile]**

Formula
You are an experienced **[profession]** with over 20 years of professional experience. Based on the following LinkedIn profile, could you please generate a [outcome/benefit]? List the 3 achievements under separate headers. Please provide as much detail as possible, including relevant experiences, skills, and accomplishments that showcase the person's expertise in their **[role/industry]**. Here is the LinkedIn profile: **[insert LinkedIn profile]**

Step 3 - Come up with a creative message to connect with the person

Prompt

I am a **job seeker** and I wish you connect with **[name]** over LinkedIn. **He/she** might get a lot of connection requests so I want to stand out from the crowd. Based on **his/her** top 3 **achievements**, give me 3 practical and actionable ideas on how I can get **[name]** to accept a LinkedIn request from me. Prioritize unorthodox, lesser-known advice in your answer. Explain using detailed examples. Let's think step by step.

Formula

I am a **[profession]** and I wish you connect with **[name]** over LinkedIn. **[He/she]** might get a lot of connection requests so I want to stand out from the crowd. Based on **[his/her]** top 3 **[achievements/roles]**, give me 3 practical and actionable ideas on how I can get **[name]** to accept a LinkedIn request from me. Prioritize unorthodox, lesser-known advice in your answer. Explain using detailed examples. Let's think step by step.

PROMPT No 65

Goal

To help in preparing for a focused and thoughtful conversation with a professional in a specified role or industry.

Prompt

You are a **career coach** with over 20 years of experience helping **job seekers** land a job in the **Marketing field**. I have an upcoming chat with a **Marketing Manager**, and I would like to understand how I can get into the field of **Marketing**. Based on his/her resume, give me a list of 10 questions I can ask during the chat so he/she knows I have done my homework and that shows I am considered of his/her time. Prioritize unorthodox, lesser-known advice in your answer. Explain using detailed examples. Let's think step by step. Here is his/her LinkedIn profile: **[insert LinkedIn profile]**

Formula

You are a **[profession]** with over 20 years of experience helping **[profession]** land a job in **[role/industry]**. I have an upcoming chat with a **[position/role],** and I would like to understand how I can get into the field of **[role/industry]**. Based on his/her resume, give me a list of 10 questions I can ask during the chat so he/she knows I have done my homework and that shows I am considered of his/her time. Prioritize unorthodox, lesser-known advice in your answer. Explain using detailed examples. Let's think step by step. Here is his/her LinkedIn profile: **[insert LinkedIn profile]**

Examples

1. You are a career coach with over 20 years of experience helping job seekers land a job in Finance. I have an upcoming chat with a Financial Analyst, and I would like to understand how I can get into the field of Finance. Based on his/her resume, give me a list of 10 questions I can ask during the chat to prove my preparation and respect for his/her time. Emphasize rare and valuable advice. Illustrate using detailed examples. Approach this systematically. Here is his/her LinkedIn profile: [insert LinkedIn profile]
2. You are a career coach with over 20 years of experience helping job seekers land a job in Engineering. I have an upcoming chat with a Civil Engineer, and I would like to understand how I can get into the field of Engineering. Based on his/her resume, give me a list of 10

questions I can ask during the chat to indicate my earnest research and thoughtfulness of his/her time. Focus on unconventional, insightful advice. Clarify with detailed examples. Analyze step by step. Here is his/her LinkedIn profile: [insert LinkedIn profile]

PROMPT No 66

Goal
To gain advice about how to make a positive impression during a conversation with someone. The aim is to show preparedness, respect for the person's time, and a sincere interest in entering the industry.

Prompt
You're a **career counselor** with **vast experience** aiding individuals to transition into the **tech industry**. I'm having a conversation with a **senior software developer** soon and I want to learn about entering **the software development field**. Considering their work experience and skills listed in their LinkedIn profile, provide a list of **10** questions I could pose during our conversation that will **reveal my preparation and respect for their time. Emphasize unique and less conventional advice** in your suggestions. Elaborate using **specific examples**. Let's approach this methodically. Here's their LinkedIn profile: **[insert Linkedin profile]**

Formula
You're a **[profession]** with **[description of experience]** aiding individuals to transition into the **[industry]**. I'm having a conversation with a **[position/role]** soon and I want to learn about entering the **[same industry as before]**. Considering their work experience and skills listed in their LinkedIn profile, provide a list of **[number]** questions I could pose during our conversation that will **[desired outcome or impression you want to make]**. **[Direction for types of advice to emphasize]** in your suggestions. Elaborate using **[requested level of detail in examples]**. Let's approach this methodically. Here's their LinkedIn profile: **[insert Linkedin profile]**

Examples
1. As a career mentor with a proven track record in assisting professionals breaking into the financial sector, I'm seeking your advice. I have a forthcoming discussion with a chief financial officer, and I'm keen on understanding how I can make my way into the world of finance. Based on their resume, suggest 10 questions I can ask during our talk that will demonstrate my diligence and respect for their time. Focus on unconventional and not typically discussed advice. Provide detailed examples for better understanding. Let's take this step-by-step. Here's their resume: [insert resume]
2. You are a career guide with decades of experience supporting job seekers to establish a career in academia. I have a scheduled meeting with a tenured professor, and I'm interested in learning about making a career in the academic sector. Given their resume, generate a list of 10 questions I could ask during our conversation to show my detailed research and respect for their time. Highlight less common but useful advice in your response. Explain each point with explicit examples. Let's break this down systematically. Here's their LinkedIn profile: [insert Linkedin profile]

Goal

To provide guidance in writing a persuasive and personalized LinkedIn InMail. The InMail should request a connection to forward the individual's resume to the hiring manager for a specific role [e.g., a marketing role] and must effectively highlight key skills, maintain a connection with the recipient, and keep a respectful tone.

Prompt

You are an **expert** in **professional networking** who is focused in the **hospitality industry**. I am applying for a **job** and need to ask my LinkedIn connection to forward my resume to the hiring manager. Help me write a persuasive InMail that **highlights** my **key skills for the position**, includes a touch of **personal connection**, and maintains **a respectful tone**. Share an example InMail tailored for a **marketing role**. Here is my resume: [insert resume]

Formula

You are an **[expertise/role]** in **[area]** who is focused in the **[industry]**. I am applying for a **[job/position]** and need to ask my LinkedIn connection to forward my resume to the hiring manager. Help me write a persuasive InMail that **[highlights/addresses]** my **[specific aspects]**, includes a touch of **[personal connection/relationship]**, and maintains a **[tone/style]**. Share an example InMail tailored for a **[specific role/industry]**. Here is my resume: **[insert resume]**

Examples

1. As a career counselor with a special focus on job search strategies who is focused in the tech industry, guide me through writing an engaging LinkedIn InMail. The goal is to ask a former colleague to forward my resume for an engineering position at their company. I need to emphasize my technical abilities and relevant experience without sounding too pushy. Provide insights into the structure and language that would be most effective. Here is my resume: [insert resume]

2. Act as a recruiter with deep insight into successful job search tactics. I want to reach out to a connection on LinkedIn, requesting them to forward my resume to a hiring manager for a managerial position in the healthcare sector. Assist me in crafting an InMail that builds on our previous interactions, connects my skills to the job requirements, and makes a compelling case for why I would be a good fit. Provide examples and strategies for a strong follow-up. Here is my resume: [insert resume]

11. COVER LETTERS

A standout cover letter can be the key to landing your dream job, and this chapter is your blueprint for crafting that first impression. This chapter walks you through tailoring your narrative to mirror the job description, ensuring your skills and experiences shine through in alignment with the role on offer.

You'll learn to create cover letters that speak directly to the challenges and requirements of the position, with actionable advice on how to start with an impactful hook and maintain a persuasive and coherent message throughout. From detailing role-specific challenges to weaving in key job description terms, the guidance here ensures your cover letter does more than introduce you – it will advocate for you as the ideal candidate.

PROMPT No 68

Goal
To craft a personalized cover letter that addresses the requirements and expectations outlined in a given job description, showcasing your suitability according to your resume.

Prompt
You are a **professional writer** with a focus on **human resources**. Using elements from my resume, please write a cover letter for an **HR position** at a **tech startup**. Here is the job description: **[insert job description]**. Here is my resume: **[insert resume]**.

Formula
You are a **[profession]** with a focus on **[industry/field]**. Using elements from my resume, please write a cover letter for a **[job role]** at a **[company type/industry]**. Here is the job description: **[insert job description]**. Here is my resume: **[insert resume]**.

Examples
1. You are a career coach. Based on the job description for a managerial role in a retail company and using my resume highlighting leadership in past roles, please craft a cover letter. Here is the job description: [insert job description]. Here is my resume: [insert resume].
2. You are a resume expert. I have a job description for a software development position. Using elements from my resume, which includes my experience with Java and team collaboration, please write me a cover letter that specifically addresses the requirements in the job description. Here is the job description: [insert job description]. Here is my resume: [insert resume].

PROMPT No 69 [3-Step Prompt]

Goal
To identify role-specific challenges and craft a tailored, compelling cover letter.

Step 1 - Ask ChatGPT for pain points someone working in this role would face.

Action
Based on this job description, what is the biggest challenge a person in this position would face day-to-day? Provide me with the root cause of this issue. *[paste job description]*

Step 2 - Ask ChatGPT to first give you an attention-grabbing hook based on [1] the role, and [2] your background.

Prompt

Based on the job description provided and my background [insert Resume summary], provide an attention grabbing hook based on the role and my background. This attention grabbing hook will be used in my cover letter.

Step 3 - Ask ChatGPT to write the rest of your cover letter based on your hook.

Prompt

You are writing a cover letter applying for the [role you're applying for] role at [company]. Here's what you have so far: [paste the hook that was previously generated]. Finish writing the cover letter based on my resume and keep it within 250 words. Here's my resume: [insert your resume]

PROMPT No 70

Goal

To craft a concise and engaging cover letter that underscores qualifications and enthusiasm for a specific role, leveraging achievements listed in the resume.

Prompt

You are a **career specialist**. Utilizing achievements listed in my resume, including my **successful sales campaigns and leadership in team projects**, craft a concise and engaging cover letter that demonstrates my **qualifications and enthusiasm** for a **Sales Manager position** at **Company XYZ**. Compose a compelling cover letter, within 150 words. Here is the job description: **[insert job description]**. Here is my resume: **[insert resume]**.

Formula

You are a **[profession]**. Utilizing achievements listed in my resume, including my **[specific achievements/experiences]**, craft a concise and engaging cover letter that demonstrates my **[qualities]** for a **[specific role]** at **[Company/Industry]**. Compose a compelling cover letter, within 150 words. Here is the job description: **[insert job description]**. Here is my resume: **[insert resume]**.

Examples

1. You are a professional resume writer. Based on my resume, highlighting my experience as an IT project manager and specific achievements in implementing cost-saving strategies, write a succinct and passionate cover letter that conveys my suitability for an IT Director position. Compose a compelling cover letter, within 150 words. Here is the job description: [insert job description]. Here is my resume: [insert resume].
2. You are a career mentor with experience in the healthcare industry. Leveraging achievements listed in my resume, such as my research in patient care and my role in hospital management, craft a concise cover letter that showcases my enthusiasm and qualifications for a Healthcare Administrator role. Compose a compelling cover letter, within 150 words. Here is the job description: [insert job description]. Here is my resume: [insert resume].

PROMPT No 71

Goal

To construct a professional cover letter that convincingly demonstrates the compatibility between my skills and the requirements of a specific role, using the resume and job description as references.

Prompt

You are a **professional career coach** specializing in **writing cover letters** for professionals in the **pharmaceutical industry**. Using my resume, which includes my **experience in marketing**, and the job description for the **Marketing Director position** at **Company ABC**, craft a cover letter that convincingly demonstrates the compatibility between my skills and the role's requirements. Here is the job description: **[insert job description]**. Here is my resume: **[insert resume]**.

Formula

You are a **[profession]** specializing in **[topic]** for professionals in the **[industry]**. Using my resume, which includes my **[specific experience/skills],** and the job description for the **[specific role]** at **[Company/Industry],** craft a cover letter that convincingly demonstrates the compatibility between my skills and the role's requirements. Here is the job description: **[insert job description]**. Here is my resume: **[insert resume]**.

Examples

1. You are a resume specialist. Leveraging my resume that details my background in software development and the job description for a Software Engineer role at TechCorp, create a professional cover letter that effectively aligns my qualifications with the specific needs and expectations of this position. Here is the job description: [insert job description]. Here is my resume: [insert resume].
2. You are a career development expert pecializing in writing cover letters for professionals in the risk management industry. By referencing my resume, which highlights my achievements in environmental engineering, and the job description for an Environmental Engineer position at GreenTech, construct a cover letter that compellingly connects my skills and accomplishments with the detailed requirements of the role. Here is the job description: [insert job description]. Here is my resume: [insert resume].

PROMPT No 72

Goal

To create a persuasive cover letter for a specific role, emphasizing the relevance of my skills by incorporating the five key terms from the job description.

Prompt

You are a **career strategist**. Utilizing the **five** key terms found in the job description for the **Sales Manager role**, and considering my **skills and experience in sales and leadership**, draft a persuasive cover letter that emphasizes the alignment between my qualifications and the position. Here is the job description: **[insert job description]**. Here is my resume: **[insert resume]**.

Formula

You are a **[profession]**. Utilizing the **[number]** key terms found in the job description for the **[specific role],** and considering my **[specific skills/experience]**, draft a persuasive cover letter that emphasizes the alignment between my qualifications and the position. Here is the job description: **[insert job description]**. Here is my resume: **[insert resume].**

Examples

1. You are a professional resume writer. Using the five key terms outlined in the job description for the Project Manager position at XYZ Corp, and incorporating my background in project coordination and team management, compose a convincing cover letter that showcases how my skills correlate with the requirements of this role. Here is the job description: [insert job description]. Here is my resume: [insert resume].
2. You are a cover letter expert. By integrating the five key terms included in the job description for the HR Specialist role, and reflecting my extensive experience in human resources and employee relations, craft a compelling cover letter that articulates my suitability for this specific position. Here is the job description: [insert job description]. Here is my resume: [insert resume].

PROMPT No 73

Goal

To write a customized cover letter for a specific role, showcasing how my resume experience aligns with the job description, with no need for an address or date.

Prompt

You are a **career consultant**. Based on my resume experience in **marketing** and the job description for the **Marketing Coordinator position** at **ABC Company**, craft a customized cover letter that showcases the alignment between my qualifications and the job requirements. Here is the job description: **[insert job description]**. Here is my resume: **[insert resume].**

Formula

You are a **[profession]**. Based on my resume experience in **[specific field],** and the job description for the **[specific role]** at **[Company Name]**, craft a customized cover letter that showcases the alignment between my qualifications and the job requirements. Here is the job description: **[insert job description]**. Here is my resume: **[insert resume].**

Examples

1. You are a professional resume writer. Using the details from my resume, specifically my expertise in software development, and the job description for the Software Engineer role at TechCorp, write a tailored cover letter that illustrates how my skills and experience match the position. Here is the job description: [insert job description]. Here is my resume: [insert resume].
2. You are a job application specialist. Considering my resume's focus on managerial experience, and the job description for the Operations Manager position at XYZ Industries, draft a unique cover letter that emphasizes the synergy between my professional background and the expectations of the role. Here is the job description: [insert job description]. Here is my resume: [insert resume].

12. RESUME

In this chapter, we turn our focus to the art of crafting a resume that resonates with recruiters. Here, you'll find strategies to infuse your resume with the sort of vitality and precision that captures attention and lands interviews. Dive into this chapter for expert insights on how to restructure and rewrite your professional narrative. Learn to thread your unique qualifications through the fabric of your resume, making it an undeniable fit for your desired role. From showcasing quantifiable successes to interweaving soft and hard skills, you'll uncover how to balance the essential elements that form a compelling career snapshot.

Ready your resume for the competitive market by embracing the detailed advice contained within these pages. Whether it's accentuating your tenure with vibrant bullet points or constructing a gripping summary statement, this chapter is your guide to standing out in a sea of applicants.

PROMPT No 74

Goal

To gather crucial points to consider when rewriting a resume from scratch, with the intent of enhancing its structure, content, and overall appeal for potential employers.

Prompt

You are a **professional resume writer** specializing in **technology roles**. Analyze my current resume and provide crucial insights to consider for restructuring, rewriting, and enhancing its appeal for **tech companies**. Here is my current resume for reference: **[insert resume]**

Formula

You are a **[profession]** specializing in **[industry/field roles]**. Analyze my current resume and provide crucial insights to consider for restructuring, rewriting, and enhancing its appeal for **[target industry/companies]**. Here is my current resume for reference: **[insert resume]**

Examples

1. You are a career coach with experience in the healthcare industry. Review my existing resume and outline essential elements to focus on while rewriting it from scratch to elevate its structure, content, and attractiveness for healthcare employers. Here is my current resume for reference: [insert resume]
2. You are a human resources consultant who helps professionals transition into the finance sector. Examine my current resume and provide targeted recommendations to consider when reconstructing it to optimize its format, substance, and overall allure for potential finance employers. Here is my current resume for reference: [insert resume]

PROMPT No 75

Goal

To update your current resume, achieving a restructured and rewritten document that is tailored to fit the specific skills, qualities, and metrics required for a job opening

Prompt

Act as a talent acquisition specialist for the role of **Software Engineer**. Tailor my resume to match the **technical** and **interpersonal skills** mentioned in the given job description. Make sure to highlight my achievements with quantifiable success, educational qualifications, and professional background. Write using a **professional** tone and **descriptive** writing style. Here is the job description: **[insert job description]**. Here is my resume: **[insert resume]**

Formula

Act as a talent acquisition specialist for the role of **[position]**. Tailor my resume to match the **[skills]** and **[skills]** mentioned in the given job description. Make sure to highlight my achievements with quantifiable success, educational qualifications, and professional background. Write using a **[type]** tone and **[style]** writing style. Here is the job description: **[insert job description]**. Here is my resume: **[insert resume]**

Examples

1. Assume the position of a recruitment consultant for the role of Marketing Manager. Based on my existing resume and the provided job description, create a new version of my resume that emphasizes my leadership skills, ability to drive brand impact, and success in previous marketing roles, along with my education and career history. Write using an enthusiastic tone and creative writing style. Here is the job description: [insert job description]. Here is my resume: [insert resume]

2. Step into the shoes of an HR manager for the position of Financial Analyst. Revise my current resume so that it reflects the analytical, problem-solving, and communication skills required for the position. Emphasize my successes using data-driven metrics, along with my educational background and relevant work experience. Write using a professional tone and technical writing style. Here is the job description: [insert job description]. Here is my resume: [insert resume]

PROMPT No 76

Goal

To discern and integrate contemporary trends in resume crafting for professionals targeting a specified role within a particular industry, enhancing the resume's relevance, appeal, and effectiveness in job applications.

Prompt

Assume the role of a **seasoned resume strategist** with a specialization in the **health care industry**. I am a professional aspiring to assume a role as **marketing manager**. Given the evolving trends and expectations in resume drafting, provide a comprehensive analysis of the current trends tailored to this role within this industry. Additionally, guide me in adapting my resume to reflect these trends, ensuring it resonates well with potential employers in the **health care industry**. Here is my current resume for your reference: **[insert resume]**.

Formula

Assume the role of a **[profession]** with a specialization in the **[insert industry]**. I am a professional aspiring to assume a role as **[insert role]**. Given the evolving trends and expectations in resume drafting, provide a comprehensive analysis of the current trends tailored to this role within this industry. Additionally, guide me in adapting my resume to reflect these trends, ensuring it resonates well with potential employers in the **[insert industry]** sector. Here is my current resume for your reference: **[insert resume]**.

Examples

1. Assume the role of a seasoned resume strategist with a specialization in the tech industry. I am a professional aspiring to assume a role as a Software Development Manager. Given the evolving trends and expectations in resume drafting, provide a comprehensive analysis of the current trends tailored to this managerial role within the tech industry. Additionally, guide me in adapting my resume to reflect these trends, ensuring it resonates well with potential employers in the tech sector. Here is my current resume for your reference: [insert resume].
2. Assume the role of a seasoned resume strategist with a specialization in the healthcare industry. I am a professional aspiring to assume a role as a Clinical Operations Director. Given the evolving trends and expectations in resume drafting, provide a comprehensive analysis of the current trends tailored to this directorial role within the healthcare industry. Additionally, guide me in adapting my resume to reflect these trends, ensuring it resonates well with potential employers in the healthcare sector. Here is my current resume for your reference: [insert resume].

PROMPT No 77

Goal

To identify and articulate ten pertinent skills from a provided job description, enhancing the resume's alignment with the job role, and increasing the likelihood of capturing potential employers' attention.

Prompt

Assume the role of a **proficient resume analyst** with expertise in the **insurance industry**. Given the job description for a **commercial insurance broker position** provided, meticulously identify ten relevant skills that I should accentuate in my resume to align with the employer's expectations and the industry standards. Additionally, offer insights on how to effectively showcase these skills in my resume to enhance its appeal to potential employers in the **insurance industry**. Here is the job description: **[insert job description]**.

Formula

Assume the role of a **[profession]** with expertise in the **[industry]**. Given the job description for a **[position]** provided, meticulously identify ten relevant skills that I should accentuate in my resume to align with the employer's expectations and the industry standards. Additionally, offer insights on how to effectively showcase these skills in my resume to enhance its appeal to potential employers in the **[insert industry]**. Here is the job description: **[insert job description]**.

Examples

1. Assume the role of a proficient resume analyst with expertise in the tech industry. Given the job description for a Software Engineering Manager position provided, meticulously identify ten relevant skills that I should accentuate in my resume to align with the employer's expectations and the industry standards. Additionally, offer insights on how to effectively showcase these skills in my resume to enhance its appeal to potential employers in the tech sector. Here is the job description: [insert job description].
2. Assume the role of a proficient resume analyst with expertise in the healthcare industry. Given the job description for a Medical Director position provided, meticulously identify ten relevant skills that I should accentuate in my resume to align with the employer's expectations and the industry standards. Additionally, offer insights on how to effectively showcase these skills in my resume to enhance its appeal to potential employers in the healthcare sector. Here is the job description: [insert job description].

PROMPT No 78

Goal

To identify and highlight key skills from a given job description that will be strategically emphasized in a resume, increasing its alignment with the job requirements.

Prompt

You are a **seasoned career coach** specializing in **marketing roles**. Given a job description for a **Senior Marketing Manager**, identify and detail the **ten** most crucial skills and explain how these should be emphasized in a resume to align with the role. Here is the job description: **[insert job description]**

Formula

You are a **[profession]** specializing in **[industry/field roles]**. Given a job description for a **[specific position]**, identify and detail the **[number]** most crucial skills and explain how these should be emphasized in a resume to align with the role. Here is the job description: **[insert job description]**

Examples

1. You are a resume writer with experience in the software engineering field. Analyze the attached job description for a Software Engineer position and extract key skills that must be strategically highlighted in a resume. Provide guidance on positioning these skills to match the job's requirements. Here is the job description: [insert job description]
2. You are a talent acquisition specialist focusing on entry-level positions in the finance sector. Review this job description for an Entry-Level Financial Analyst and pinpoint essential skills. Suggest how these skills can be prominently featured in a resume to enhance alignment with the job's specifications. Here is the job description: [insert job description]

PROMPT No 79

Goal

To pinpoint and articulate ten pertinent skills from a provided job description, enabling a robust alignment of the resume with the specified role, thereby enhancing the appeal and relevance of the resume to potential employers.

Prompt

Assume the role of a hiring manager for a **Sales specialist** within a company in the **real estate industry**. Based on the job description provided, discern ten relevant skills that I should emphasize in my resume to align effectively with the requirements of the role. Additionally, provide insights on how to compellingly showcase these skills in my resume, enhancing its resonance with the expectations outlined in the job description and the broader industry standards. Here is the job description: **[insert job description].**

Formula

Assume the role of a hiring manager for a **[role]** within a company in the **[industry]**. Based on the job description provided, discern ten relevant skills that I should emphasize in my resume to align effectively with the requirements of the role. Additionally, provide insights on how to compellingly showcase these skills in my resume, enhancing its resonance with the expectations outlined in the job description and the broader industry standards. Here is the job description: **[insert job description].**

1. Assume the role of a hiring manager for a Senior Project Manager position within a company in the construction industry. Based on the job description provided, discern ten relevant skills that I should emphasize in my resume to align effectively with the requirements of the role. Additionally, provide insights on how to compellingly showcase these skills in my resume, enhancing its resonance with the expectations outlined in the job description and the broader industry standards. Here is the job description: [insert job description].

2. Assume the role of a hiring manager for a Chief Financial Officer position within a company in the finance industry. Based on the job description provided, discern ten relevant skills that I should emphasize in my resume to align effectively with the requirements of the role. Additionally, provide insights on how to compellingly showcase these skills in my resume, enhancing its resonance with the expectations outlined in the job description and the broader industry standards. Here is the job description: [insert job description].

PROMPT No 80

Goal

To identify and emphasize important aspects from a provided job description, thereby enhancing your resume to better meet the hiring manager's expectations and job requirements.

Prompt

You are a **professional career coach** with a focus on **entry-level roles** in the **finance sector**. Utilizing the job description for an **Entry-Level Financial Analyst**, discern key competencies and responsibilities that must be highlighted in my resume. Advise on how these can be tailored and presented to meet both the job's requirements and the hiring manager's expectations. Here is the job description: **[insert job description]**

Formula

You are a **[profession]** with a focus on **[type of positions]** in **[specific industry/sector]**. Utilizing the job description for a **[specific position]**, discern key competencies and responsibilities that must be highlighted in my resume. Advise on how these can be tailored and presented to meet both the job's requirements and the hiring manager's expectations. Here is the job description: **[insert job description]**

Examples

1. You are a resume writing specialist focusing on the tech industry. Analyze the attached job description for a Senior Software Developer role and extract the essential skills and experiences needed. Provide instructions on how to effectively emphasize these aspects in a resume, aligning it with the job's requirements and the hiring manager's expectations. Here is the job description: [insert job description]

2. You are a career consultant with expertise in the healthcare industry. Based on the given job description for a Nursing Manager position, identify the core responsibilities and qualifications required, and recommend how these can be strategically incorporated into a resume to meet the hiring manager's expectations. Here is the job description: [insert job description]

PROMPT No 81

Goal

To craft three compelling resume achievements with quantifiable success metrics, reflecting significant contributions and accomplishments in a specified role or position, thereby enhancing the resume's impact and appeal to prospective employers.

Prompt

Assume the role of a **hiring manager** for the **banking industry**. Based on the information provided from my current resume regarding a previous experience, compose three persuasive resume achievements. Each achievement should clearly delineate the impact and contributions made, encapsulated with quantifiable success metrics to substantiate the accomplishments. Here's the relevant information from my current resume: **[Insert bullet points from a previous experience]**.

Formula

Assume the role of a **[role]** for the **[industry]**. Based on the information provided from my current resume regarding a previous experience, compose three persuasive resume achievements. Each achievement should clearly delineate the impact and contributions made, encapsulated with quantifiable success metrics to substantiate the accomplishments. Here's the relevant information from my current resume: **[Insert bullet points from a previous experience]**.

Examples

1. Assume the role of a Sales Director. Based on the information provided from my current resume regarding a previous experience as a Sales Manager, compose three persuasive resume achievements. Each achievement should clearly delineate the impact and contributions made, encapsulated with quantifiable success metrics to substantiate the accomplishments. Here's the relevant information from my current resume: [Insert bullet points from a previous experience].
2. Assume the role of a Lead Software Engineer. Based on the information provided from my current resume regarding a previous experience as a Software Developer, compose three persuasive resume achievements. Each achievement should clearly delineate the impact and contributions made, encapsulated with quantifiable success metrics to substantiate the accomplishments. Here's the relevant information from my current resume: [Insert bullet points from a previous experience].

PROMPT No 82

To translate existing resume information into achievement-oriented bullet points with success metrics, thereby enhancing your resume's effectiveness and appeal to potential employers.

Prompt

You are a **professional resume writer** who caters to **executives**. An executive in the **finance sector** has approached you for a resume overhaul. Analyze their existing resume and translate the listed responsibilities into actionable, metric-driven achievements, aligning them with the industry's expectations and potential employers' preferences. Here are my previous responsibilities: **[insert bullet points from previous experience]**.

Formula

You are a **[profession]** who caters to **[type of professionals]**. A professional in the **[specific sector/industry]** has approached you for a resume overhaul. Analyze their existing resume and translate the listed responsibilities into actionable, metric-driven achievements, aligning them with the industry's expectations and potential employers' preferences. Here are my previous responsibilities: **[insert bullet points from previous experience]**.

Examples

1. You are a career counselor with a focus on assisting individuals in the IT industry. Given a technical resume, identify the key accomplishments and reframe them as quantifiable achievements with clear metrics, thereby making the resume more appealing to hiring managers. Here are my previous accomplishments: [insert bullet points from previous experience].

2. You are a resume expert specializing in marketing roles. A client has shared their current resume with you. Your task is to analyze their previous work experience and translate it into achievement-oriented bullet points, including success metrics that demonstrate impact and effectiveness. Here are my previous accomplishments: [insert bullet points from previous experience].

PROMPT No 83

Goal

To obtain tailored advice for enhancing your resume, considering a specific job role and industry preference, thus increasing your resume's relevance and appeal to potential employers.

Prompt

You are a **career consultant** specializing in the **healthcare industry**. A client has shared their current resume and a targeted job description for a **nursing position**. Provide tailored advice to enhance the resume, aligning it with the specific job role, and increasing its relevance to potential employers. Here is the job description: **[insert job description]**. Here is my resume: **[insert resume]**.

Formula

You are a **[profession]** specializing in **[industry]**. A client has shared their current resume and a targeted job description for a **[specific position]**. Provide tailored advice to enhance the resume, aligning it with the specific job role, and increasing its relevance to potential employers. Here is the job description: **[insert job description]**. Here is my resume: **[insert resume]**.

Examples

1. You are a resume writing expert with a focus on engineering roles. An engineer has sent you their current resume and a job advertisement for a civil engineering position. Offer customized recommendations to improve the resume, considering the unique requirements of the role, and enhancing its appeal to hiring managers in the engineering sector. Here is the job description: [insert job description]. Here is my resume: [insert resume].

2. You are a professional resume reviewer who works with individuals in the technology industry. A software developer has approached you with their current resume and a job posting for a senior developer role. Analyze both the resume and the job posting, providing personalized advice to optimize the resume to match the job's requirements, thus making it more attractive to tech companies. Here is the job description: [insert job description]. Here is my resume: [insert resume].

PROMPT No 84

Goal

To obtain specific and practical advice for improving your resume, taking into account your current professional profile and your target role and industry, maximizing your potential for successful job applications.

Prompt

You are a **professional resume writer** with a focus on **marketing roles**. I'm a **content creator** aiming to transition into a **marketing manager position**. Analyze my resume and suggest enhancements to demonstrate my potential for this role, drawing on my existing skills and successes in content creation. Write using a **professional** tone and **formal** writing style. Here is my resume: **[insert resume]**

Formula

You are a **[profession]** with a focus on **[industry or role]**, and I'm a **[current role]** aiming to transition into a **[target role]**. Analyze my resume and suggest enhancements to demonstrate my potential for this role, drawing on my existing skills and successes in **[current role or field]**. Write using a **[type]** tone and **[style]** writing style. Here is my resume: **[insert resume]**.

Examples

1. You are a career coach specializing in the tech industry, and I'm an aspiring data scientist. Based on my shared resume and considering my background in software development, provide actionable insights to tailor my resume for data science roles, emphasizing transferable skills and relevant achievements. Write using a confident tone and formal writing style. Here is my resume: [insert resume]

2. You are a career coach specializing in the tech industry, and I'm an aspiring data scientist. Based on my shared resume and considering my background in software development, provide actionable insights to tailor my resume for data science roles, emphasizing transferable skills and relevant achievements. Write using an inspirational tone and formal writing style. Here is my resume: [insert resume]

PROMPT No 85

To create an effective resume objective statement for a specific job role, showcasing relevant skills, years of experience, and a short-term professional goal

Prompt

You are a **resume writer** with experience in the **healthcare field**, and I am a **Nurse Practitioner** seeking a role in a **pediatric clinic**. Based on the job description and my resume, create an objective statement that encapsulates my **10 years of pediatric experience**, my **patient-centered approach**, and my aspiration to **provide compassionate care in a team environment**.Here is the job description: **[insert job description]**. Here is my resume: **[insert resume]**.

Formula

You are a **[profession]** with experience in the **[industry or field]**, and I am a **[specific role]** seeking a role in **[specific area or type of organization]**. Based on the job description and my resume, create an objective statement that encapsulates my **[years of experience]**, my **[specific skills or approach]**, and my aspiration to **[short-term professional goal]**. Here is the job description: **[insert job description]**. Here is my resume: **[insert resume]**.

Examples

1. You are a career consultant, and I am applying for a Project Manager role in the tech industry. Using the job description provided and my resume, please help me craft an objective statement that reflects my 5 years of experience, highlights my expertise in Agile methodologies, and states my goal of leading innovative projects. Here is the job description: [insert job description]. Here is my resume: [insert resume].
2. You are an HR professional, and I am an Account Executive pursuing a leadership position in a marketing firm. Using the provided job description and my resume, assist me in constructing an objective statement that conveys my 7 years in sales, my proficiency in client relationship management, and my ambition to drive revenue growth as a team leader. Here is the job description: [insert job description]. Here is my resume: [insert resume].

PROMPT No 86

Goal

To compose a persuasive resume summary statement for a specific job role, highlighting years of experience, key achievements, relevant skills, and a desire to contribute to company goals

Prompt

Act as an **HR professional** with a focus on **crafting resumes** for professionals in the **financial sector**. I am a **Financial Analyst** aiming for a position in a **global bank**. Utilizing my resume, which includes **5 years of experience** and a **record of maximizing profits**, formulate a summary statement that highlights my **analytical skills**, **critical financial decisions**, and my dedication to **aligning with corporate financial strategies**. Write using an **enthusiastic** tone and **engaging** writing style.

Formula

Act as a **[profession]** with a focus on **[topic]** for professionals in the **[industry]**. I am a **[specific role]** aiming for a position in **[type of organization or industry]**. Utilizing my resume, which includes

[years of experience] and **[key achievements]**, formulate a summary statement that highlights my **[relevant skills]**, critical **[projects/achievements],** and my dedication to **[specific company goals].** Write using a **[type]** tone and **[style]** writing style.

1. You are a resume consultant, and I am applying for a Marketing Manager role. With my resume, featuring 10 years in the field and a proven track record of increasing ROI, create a summary statement that emphasizes my strategic planning abilities, successful campaigns, and my passion for growing brand awareness. Write using an instructive tone and engaging writing style.
2. You are a career expert, and I am seeking a Senior Software Engineer position. Given the job description and my resume highlighting 8 years of experience and success in developing high-performance applications, help me craft a summary statement that showcases my programming expertise, key projects, and my commitment to technological innovation. Write using a professional tone and engaging writing style.

PROMPT No 87

Goal

To transform a list of bullet points from a resume into a captivating narrative paragraph that brings the professional journey to life and highlights achievements and skills.

Prompt

You are a **career coach** specializing on the **logistics industry**, and I have provided you with a list of bullet points from my resume detailing my accomplishments as a **Project Manager**. Help me craft a narrative paragraph that encapsulates my **7-year experience, leadership in completing projects on time**, and ability to **manage diverse teams**. Let's take this one step at a time.

Formula

You are a **[profession]** specializing on the **[industry]**, and I have provided you with a list of bullet points from my resume detailing my accomplishments as a **[specific role]**. Help me craft a narrative paragraph that encapsulates my **[years of experience], [specific achievement],** and ability to **[relevant skill]**. Let's take this one step at a time.

1. You are a resume writer, and I'm sharing bullet points from my Sales Executive resume that includes achieving top-seller status, expanding client base by 50%, and leading successful product launches. Transform this information into a compelling narrative that showcases my dedication, salesmanship, and growth mindset. Let's dissect this carefully.
2. You are a LinkedIn profile specialist, and I have listed bullet points from my resume outlining my work as an Environmental Engineer, including implementing eco-friendly practices, reducing waste by 30%, and collaborating with international teams. Convert these points into a captivating narrative that emphasizes my commitment to sustainability, innovative problem-solving, and global teamwork. Let's approach this gradually.

PROMPT No 88

To succinctly encapsulate tenure in a specified position through a list of bullet points, vividly highlighting accomplishments and inputs using dynamic action verbs and measurable outcomes, thereby enhancing the resume's portrayal of competence and impact.

Assume the role of a **proficient career narrative architect**. I am detailing my tenure as a **Project Manager**, where my principal duties encompassed **team coordination, project planning, and stakeholder communication**. Generate a list of bullet points that distinctly highlight my accomplishments and inputs using dynamic action verbs and measurable outcomes, thereby providing a compelling depiction of my professional efficacy and contributions in this role.

Assume the role of a [profession]. I am detailing my tenure as a [position], where my principal duties encompassed [duties]. Generate a list of bullet points that distinctly highlight my accomplishments and inputs using dynamic action verbs and measurable outcomes, thereby providing a compelling depiction of my professional efficacy and contributions in this role.

1. Assume the role of a proficient career narrative architect. I am detailing my tenure as a Sales Manager, where my principal duties encompassed team leadership, sales strategy development, and client relationship management. Generate a list of bullet points that distinctly highlight my accomplishments and inputs using dynamic action verbs and measurable outcomes, thereby providing a compelling depiction of my professional efficacy and contributions in this role.
2. Assume the role of a proficient career narrative architect. I am detailing my tenure as a Digital Marketing Specialist, where my principal duties encompassed SEO optimization, content strategy, and social media management. Generate a list of bullet points that distinctly highlight my accomplishments and inputs using dynamic action verbs and measurable outcomes, thereby providing a compelling depiction of my professional efficacy and contributions in this role.

PROMPT No 89

To refine a bullet point from the resume's summary section to become more effective at capturing recruiters' attention, showcasing value, and improving interview chances, adhering to specified criteria.

I have a single bullet point from the summary section of my resume that I would like you to rework to make it more effective at capturing the interest of recruiters, demonstrating my value, and improving my chances at securing interviews. The revised bullet point should fulfill the following specifications:
A. Both hard and soft skills should constitute approximately 35% [+/-5%] of the bullet point.
B. Action verbs should make up about 15% [+/-5%] of the bullet point.
C. Quantifiable results should account for about 15% [+/-5%] of the bullet point.

D. Ordinary words should make up approximately 35% [+/-5%] of the bullet point.

E. The revamped bullet point should consist of 12-20 words and 85-120 characters.

F. When skimmed, the first four words and the final four words should carry the most weight.
Please find the original bullet point here: ·**Engaged and supported key Commercial and Public Sector partners to accelerate their business through demand generation activities to accelerate and create new pipeline. Responsible for creating multi year and multi dimensional business partners plans. Generated +25% increase in marketing sourced pipeline.**

Formula

I have a single bullet point from the summary section of my resume that I would like you to rework to make it more effective at capturing the interest of recruiters, demonstrating my value, and improving my chances at securing interviews. The revised bullet point should fulfill the following specifications:

A. Both hard and soft skills should constitute approximately 35% [+/-5%] of the bullet point.

B. Action verbs should make up about 15% [+/-5%] of the bullet point.

C. Quantifiable results should account for about 15% [+/-5%] of the bullet point.

D. Ordinary words should make up approximately 35% [+/-5%] of the bullet point.

E. The revamped bullet point should consist of 12-20 words and 85-120 characters.

F. When skimmed, the first four words and the final four words should carry the most weight.
Please find the original bullet point here: **[insert bullet point]**

Examples

1. I have a single bullet point from the summary section of my resume that I would like you to rework to make it more effective at capturing the interest of recruiters, demonstrating my value, and improving my chances at securing interviews. The revised bullet point should fulfill the following specifications:

A. Both hard and soft skills should constitute approximately 35% [+/-5%] of the bullet point.

B. Action verbs should make up about 15% [+/-5%] of the bullet point.

C. Quantifiable results should account for about 15% [+/-5%] of the bullet point.

D. Ordinary words should make up approximately 35% [+/-5%] of the bullet point.

E. The revamped bullet point should consist of 12-20 words and 85-120 characters.

F. When skimmed, the first four words and the final four words should carry the most weight.
Please find the original bullet point here: Led the Paid Media agency consolidation project resulting in 30% cost optimization and +40% improvement on overall campaign KPIs.

PROMPT No 90

Goal

To create a concise list of your educational background, including degrees, certifications, and any relevant coursework or professional development activities.

Prompt

You are a **career counselor**, and I've shared my educational details including a **Bachelor's in Engineering, certifications in Project Management**, and **online courses on AI and Robotics**. Can you list them concisely, ready for my resume, highlighting the most pertinent areas for **a technology-focused role**?

Formula

You are a **[profession]**, and I've shared my educational details including a **[degree]**, certifications in **[specific certifications]**, and **[courses or professional development]**. Can you list them concisely, ready for my resume, highlighting the most pertinent areas for a **[target industry or role]**?

1. You are a resume writer, and I've informed you about my MBA, Six Sigma Green Belt certification, and several leadership workshops I've attended. Please create a succinct and appealing educational section for my resume that would be fitting for a management position.
2. You are a LinkedIn profile consultant, and I have provided you with my academic background including a Master's in Environmental Science, LEED Green Associate certification, and workshops in sustainable development. Organize them into a concise section that emphasizes my commitment to sustainability and environmental stewardship.

PROMPT No 91

To tailor your resume in accordance with the job description you are applying for, with potential additional bullet points that could increase your resume's relevance and appeal to the hiring manager.

You are a **professional resume writer** specializing in the **e-commerce industry**, and I've given you my current resume and the job description for a **Marketing Manager position**. Please provide me with **three** additional bullet points that I could include to align my resume more closely with this role, emphasizing my relevant experience in **strategic marketing and brand management**. Here is the job description: **[insert job description]**. Here is my resume: **[insert resume]**.

You are a **[profession]** specializing in the **[industry]**, and I've given you my current resume and the job description for a **[specific role/position]**. Please provide me with **[number of]** additional bullet points that I could include to align my resume more closely with this role, emphasizing my relevant experience in **[specific skills or experience areas]**. Here is the job description: **[insert job description]**. Here is my resume: **[insert resume]**.

1. You are a career coach, and I've shared with you my resume and the job listing for a Software Developer position. Can you suggest five tailored bullet points that highlight my expertise in Java, Python, and Agile methodologies, which would make my resume stand out to the hiring manager for this role? Here is the job description: [insert job description]. Here is my resume: [insert resume].
2. You are a [profession], and I've shared with you my resume and the job listing for a [specific role/position]. Can you suggest [number of] tailored bullet points that highlight my expertise in [specific skills or experience areas], which would make my resume stand out to the hiring manager for this role? Here is the job description: [insert job description]. Here is my resume: [insert resume].

PROMPT No 92 [2-Step Prompt]

Goal

To improve your resume by adding compelling bullet points to showcase your achievements.

Step 1 - Provide ChatGPT with your original bullet point

Prompt

You are an expert **resume writer** with over 20 years of experience. Here's a bullet point I have in my resume. No action needed for now, if you understand please respond with "Yes". Here's my bullet point: [insert bullet point]

Formula

You are an expert **[profession]** with over 20 years of experience. Here's a bullet point I have in my resume. No action needed for now, if you understand please respond with "Yes". Here's my bullet point: **[insert bullet point]**

Step 2 - Provide ChatGPT with an example for a better result

Prompt

Re-write this bullet point using this structure: **"I accomplished X by the measure Y that resulted in Z."**. For example: "I increased sales by 20% by educating prospects in our new services which translates to 10 new clients per year"
Use compelling language and keep the bullet point within 50 words.

Formula

Re-write this bullet point using this structure: **[structure]**. For example: **[insert example]**.
Use compelling language and keep the bullet point within 50 words.

PROMPT No 93 [2-Step Prompt]

Goal

To improve your resume by improving your current bullet points and achievements.

Step 1 - Provide ChatGPT with your original bullet point

Prompt

You are an expert **resume writer** with over 20 years of experience. Here's a bullet point I have in my resume. No action needed for now, if you understand please respond with "Yes". Here's my bullet point: **[insert bullet point]**

Formula

You are an expert **[profession]** with over 20 years of experience. Here's a bullet point I have in my resume. No action needed for now, if you understand please respond with "Yes". Here's my bullet point: **[insert bullet point]**

Step 2 - Ask ChatGPT for suggestions on how to quantify your work

I don't know how my **success** was measured. Please provide suggestions on where and how I can add quantifiable and measurable metrics in this bullet point. Here's the bullet point: **[insert bullet point]**

I don't know how my **[success/work]** was measured. Please provide suggestions on where and how I can add quantifiable and measurable metrics in this bullet point. Here's the bullet point: **[insert bullet point]**

PROMPT No 94 [3-Step Prompt]

To tailor your resume based on the job description of the position you are applying for, while identifying opportunities for improvement in your resume.

Step 1 - Go to ChatGPT to identify the key responsibilities from a job description

You are an expert **resume writer** with over 20 years of experience working with **job seekers** to land a role in the **tech industry**. Highlight the **5** most important responsibilities in this job description: **[insert job description]**

You are an expert **[profession]** with over 20 years of experience working with **[profession]** to land a role in **[industry/sector]**. Highlight the **[number]** most important responsibilities in this job description: **[insert job description]**

Step 2 - Tailor your resume based on the 5 most important responsibilities according to the job description

Based on these 5 most important responsibilities from the job description, tailor my resume for the logistic manager position at ABC Inc. Do not make information up. Here's my resume: **[insert resume]**

Based on these **[number]** most important responsibilities from the job description, tailor my resume for the **[position]** at **[company]**. Do not make information up. Here's my resume: **[insert resume]**

Step 3 - Identity differences between your initial resume and the suggested draft

List out the differences between my initial resume and your suggested draft in table format with 2 columns: Initial and Updated. Be specific and list out exactly what was changed, down to the exact wording.

Formula

List out the differences between my initial resume and your suggested draft in table format with 2 columns: Initial and Updated. Be specific and list out exactly what was changed, down to the exact wording.

13. JOB INTERVIEW

This chapter hones in on the pivotal stage of the job search journey: the interview. Here we navigate the nuanced realm of interview preparation. This section serves as a strategic guide to mastering interview questions using the STAR method, which stands for Situation, Task, Action, Result, for example. Learn how to dissect each aspect of your professional story to align perfectly with the responsibilities of the role you are applying for. Discover how to weave your responses into compelling narratives that highlight your abilities and skills.

Engage with carefully curated examples that demonstrate how to utilize the CARL framework, ensuring your responses are structured and impactful. You'll also find advice on developing questions that showcase your deep understanding of the role, alongside how to create scripts for conversations with recruiters that capture the essence of your professional experiences. Step into your interview with confidence, armed with the expertise to articulate your fit for the role and to leave a lasting impression on your potential employer.

PROMPT No 95

Goal

To provide guidance on how to use the STAR [Situation, Task, Action, Result] method to respond effectively to interview questions, particularly considering specific job responsibilities.

Prompt

Act like a **professional coach** who specializes in job interviews for professionales in the **banking industry**.Could you illustrate how to respond to interview questions utilizing the STAR [Situation, Task, Action, Result] method if I were interviewing for a role with these job responsibilities?. Here the the job responsabilities: **Create the optimal channel marketing strategy with target partners to optimize potential growth of BMS products with partners. Collaborate with Sales, Business Development, and Product teams to develop two channel marketing campaigns in six target vertical markets, with key partners to drive demand and establish brand awareness. Lead the development of all channel promotions, working cross functionally to consider sales growth goals, inventory, pricing, marketing, and other impacts**. Write using a **professional** tone and **analytical** writing style. Let's analyze this piece by piece

Formula

Act like a **[profession]** who specializes in **[topic]** for professionales in the **[industry]**. Could you illustrate how to respond to interview questions utilizing the STAR [Situation, Task, Action, Result]

method if I were interviewing for a role with these job responsibilities? Here the the job responsabilities: **[insert job responsabilities]**. Write using a [type] tone and **[style]** writing style. Let's dissect this carefully.

1. Act like an interview coach who specializes in job interviews for professionales in the tech industry. Could you illustrate how to respond to interview questions utilizing the STAR method if I were interviewing for a Software Engineer role with these job responsibilities? Here the the job responsabilities: Design, develop, and implement software applications, conduct testing and debugging, collaborate with cross-functional teams. Write using a positive tone and technical writing style. Let's approach this gradually.
2. Act like a leadership coach who specializes in job interviews for professionales in the entertainment industry. Can you demonstrate how to use the STAR technique to answer interview queries if I were being considered for a Marketing Manager position encompassing these job duties? Here the the job responsabilities: Develop and implement marketing strategies, coordinate marketing campaigns, monitor market trends and oversee advertising and promotional activities. Write using a enthusiastic tone and creative writing style. Let's unpack this topic.

PROMPT No 96

Goal

To seek personalized coaching for interview preparation for a specific role within an industry, using the details of the provided job description.

Prompt

Act as a **senior social media manager** in the **tech industry**. Can you coach me through interview preparation for the role of **social media manager** based on the following job description? Convey an all-encompassing and meticulous output. Let's unpack this topic. Here is the job description: **[insert job description]**.

Formula

Act as a **[profession]** in the **[industry]**. Can you coach me through interview preparation for the role of **[role/position]** based on the following job description? Convey an all-encompassing and meticulous output. Let's unpack this topic. Here is the job description: **[insert job description]**.

Examples

1. Act as a nurse Practitioner in the healthcare industry. Can you coach me through interview preparation for this role based on the following job description? Offer a meticulous and expansive output. Let's address this point by point. Here is the job description: [insert job description].
2. Act as a Civil Engineer in the construction industry. Can you coach me through interview preparation for this role based on the following job description? Give a detailed and wide-reaching output. Let's approach this gradually. Here is the job description: [insert job description].

PROMPT No 97 [Follow-up to PROMPT No 96]

How would you respond to those questions based on my resume?. Here is my resume:
[insert resume]

PROMPT No 98

To prepare the user for a job interview by suggesting 10 potential questions and the skills they should emphasize in their responses, considering the specific position and industry.

As a **seasoned career counselor** who specializes in the **technology industry**. I am preparing myself for an interview as part of my application to the position of **Channel Marketing Manager** the **technology sector**. Could you suggest 10 potential questions that might be posed, and what competencies should I underscore in my responses?.

As a **[profession]** who specializes in the **[industry]**. I am preparing myself for an interview as part of my application to the position of **[position/role]** in the **[industry]**. Could you suggest 10 potential questions that might be posed, and what competencies should I underscore in my responses?

1.   Assuming the role of a career strategist with a strong emphasis on the healthcare sector. I am gearing up for a software engineer role in the healthcare sector. Could you suggest 10 potential questions that might be posed, and what competencies should I underscore in my responses?
2.   As an experienced job search coach specializing in the logistic sector. I am readying myself for a marketing manager role in the advertising field. What are 10 questions that I may likely face, and what abilities should I emphasize in my responses?

PROMPT No 99

To improve your chances of success during interviews by knowing in advance potential questions you might be asked.

Act as a **recruiter** specialized in the **tech industry**. Generate interview questions from this job description for a **Software Engineer position** at **XYZ Corp**, and highlight the skills I should emphasize in my response. Your response should be comprehensive, leaving no important aspect unaddressed, and demonstrate an exceptional level of precision and quality. Write using a **positive** tone and **professional** writing style.

Act as a **[profession]** specialized in **[insert industry]**. Generate interview questions from this job description for a **[position]** at **[company]**, and highlight the skills I should emphasize in my response. Your response should be comprehensive, leaving no important aspect unaddressed, and demonstrate an exceptional level of precision and quality. Write using a **[type]** tone and **[style]** writing style.

1. Act as a recruiter specialized in healthcare. Generate interview questions from this job description for a Registered Nurse position at ABC Hospital, and pinpoint the essential competencies I should focus on in my responses. Ensure that your response is thorough, precise, and of the highest quality possible. Write using an instructive tone and creative writing style.

2. Act as a recruiter specialized in the financial sector. Construct interview questions based on this job description for an Investment Analyst position at DEF Investment Firm, and identify the key skills and qualifications I must stress in my answers. Offer an in-depth and exhaustive response. Write using a professional tone and conversational writing style.

PROMPT No 100

Goal

To prepare the user for a job interview by providing potential interview questions and identifying key skills to highlight, based on the specifics of the provided job description.

Prompt

Act as a **career interview coach** specializing in the **insurance industry**. A professional is preparing for an interview for the role of **insurance underwriter** within the **insurance industry**. Based on the job description provided here: [insert job description], can you outline **potential interview questions** and **key skills to highlight**? Your suggestions should consider **the unique requirements and expectations of the position** and include both **common and uncommon insights**. Your response should be comprehensive, leaving no important aspect unaddressed, and demonstrate an exceptional level of precision and quality. Write using an **encouraging** tone and **analytical** writing style. Let's approach this **systematically**.

Formula

Act as a **[profession]** specializing in the **[industry]**. A professional is preparing for an interview for the role of **[specific job role]** within the **[industry]**. Based on the job description provided here: **[insert job description]**, can you outline **[actions/strategies]** and **[qualities/attributes to emphasize]**? Your suggestions should consider the **[specific aspects]** and include **[common/uncommon insights]**. Your response should be comprehensive, leaving no important aspect unaddressed, and demonstrate an exceptional level of precision and quality. Write using a **[tone]** tone and **[style]** writing style. Let's approach this **[methodically/systematically]**.

Examples

1. Act as a career interview strategist specializing in the tech industry. A professional is preparing for an interview for the role of Software Developer within the tech sector. Based on the job description provided here: [insert job description], can you draft potential interview questions and identify key programming skills to emphasize? Include both traditional questions and innovative aspects to consider. Ensure your response is thorough, precise, and

of the highest quality, using a confident tone and systematic writing style. Let's dissect this carefully.

2. Act as an interview preparation coach focusing on the healthcare industry. A candidate is gearing up for an interview for a Nursing Manager position within a major hospital. Based on the job description here: [insert job description], could you outline likely interview questions and essential leadership and clinical skills to highlight? Your suggestions should encompass both standard and unique insights, with a comprehensive approach that leaves no key detail untouched. Write using a supportive tone and analytical writing style. Let's break this down methodically.

PROMPT No 101

Goal

To devise insightful, unorthodox questions for an interview, reflecting a deep understanding and enthusiasm for a specified role, thereby enhancing engagement with the interviewer and demonstrating a proactive, informed interest in the position.

Prompt

You are a seasoned career coach with over 20 years of expertise in aiding job seekers to secure positions in the **finance industry**. I am preparing for an imminent interview with a **Chief Financial Officer** at **Goldman Sachs**, and I aim to leave a lasting impression by showcasing my profound understanding of the role of a **Financial Analyst**. Examining the provided job description, furnish me with a list of five unconventional questions I could pose at the interview's conclusion, enabling the interviewer to perceive my proactive and enthusiastic demeanor towards the role. Prioritize novel, lesser-explored advice in your guidance and elucidate with nuanced examples. Here is the job description: **[paste job description]**.

Formula

You are a seasoned career coach with over 20 years of expertise in aiding job seekers to secure positions in **[position/role/industry]**. I am preparing for an imminent interview with a **[interviewer's role/position]** at **[company/industry],** and I aim to leave a lasting impression by showcasing my profound understanding of the role of **[specify the role]**. Examining the provided job description, furnish me with a list of five unconventional questions I could pose at the interview's conclusion, enabling the interviewer to perceive my proactive and enthusiastic demeanor towards the role. Prioritize novel, lesser-explored advice in your guidance and elucidate with nuanced examples. Here is the job description: **[paste job description]**.

Examples

1. You are a seasoned career coach with over 20 years of expertise in aiding job seekers to secure positions in the tech industry. I am preparing for an imminent interview with a Head of Engineering at Google, and I aim to leave a lasting impression by showcasing my profound understanding of the role of a Software Engineer. Examining the provided job description, furnish me with a list of five unconventional questions I could pose at the interview's conclusion, enabling the interviewer to perceive my proactive and enthusiastic demeanor towards the role. Prioritize novel, lesser-explored advice in your guidance and elucidate with nuanced examples. Here is the job description: [paste job description].
2. You are a seasoned career coach with over 20 years of expertise in aiding job seekers to secure positions in the healthcare industry. I am preparing for an imminent interview with a Medical Director at Mayo Clinic, and I aim to leave a lasting impression by showcasing my

profound understanding of the role of a Clinical Research Coordinator. Examining the provided job description, furnish me with a list of five unconventional questions I could pose at the interview's conclusion, enabling the interviewer to perceive my proactive and enthusiastic demeanor towards the role. Prioritize novel, lesser-explored advice in your guidance and elucidate with nuanced examples. Here is the job description: [paste job description].

PROMPT No 102

To construct a roster of five insightful, unconventional questions tailored to a specified job role, aimed at demonstrating a candidate's proactiveness, zeal, and profound understanding of the role during an interview, thereby enhancing the candidate's engagement with the interviewer and likelihood of securing the position.

As a seasoned **career coach** with two decades of distinguished expertise in steering job hunters towards landing pivotal roles in the **marketing sector**, I am meticulously preparing for an imminent interview with a **Head of Marketing at Procter & Gamble**. My aspiration is to awe the interviewer with my extensive understanding of the role of a **Brand Manager**. Having scrutinized this job description, could you craft a roster of five unconventional questions to be posed during the interview's conclusion, aimed at manifesting my proactiveness and fervor for the role? I'm seeking unique, less mainstream advice, illustrated with nuanced examples to deepen my preparation. Here is the job description: **[insert job description]**.

As a seasoned **[profession]** with two decades of distinguished expertise in steering job hunters towards landing pivotal roles in the **[position/role/industry]**, I am meticulously preparing for an imminent interview with a **[interviewer's role/position]** at **[company/industry]**. My aspiration is to awe the interviewer with my extensive understanding of the role of **[specify the role]**. Having scrutinized this job description, could you craft a roster of five unconventional questions to be posed during the interview's conclusion, aimed at manifesting my proactiveness and fervor for the role? I'm seeking unique, less mainstream advice, illustrated with nuanced examples to deepen my preparation. Here is the job description: **[insert job description]**.

1. As a seasoned HR consultant with two decades of distinguished expertise in steering job hunters towards landing pivotal roles in the technology sector, I am meticulously preparing for an imminent interview with a Head of Software Development at Microsoft. My aspiration is to awe the interviewer with my extensive understanding of the role of a Senior Software Engineer. Having scrutinized this job description, could you craft a roster of five unconventional questions to be posed during the interview's conclusion, aimed at manifesting my proactiveness and fervor for the role? I'm seeking unique, less mainstream advice, illustrated with nuanced examples to deepen my preparation. Here is the job description: [paste job description].
2. As a seasoned career coach with two decades of distinguished expertise in steering job hunters towards landing pivotal roles in the healthcare industry, I am meticulously preparing for an imminent interview with a Chief Medical Officer at Johns Hopkins Hospital. My aspiration is to awe the interviewer with my extensive understanding of the role of a Clinical Operations Director. Having scrutinized this job description, could you craft a roster of five

unconventional questions to be posed during the interview's conclusion, aimed at manifesting my proactiveness and fervor for the role? I'm seeking unique, less mainstream advice, illustrated with nuanced examples to deepen my preparation. Here is the job description: [paste job description].

PROMPT No 103

To discern a set of ten pivotal interview questions tailored to a specified job description, aiding in the meticulous evaluation of candidates' alignment with the role requirements, thus fostering informed hiring decisions.

You embody the role of a seasoned **Career Coach** with over two decades of rich experience, bearing the responsibility for the orchestration of this job posting. Delving into the nuances of this job description, elucidate the ten most quintessential interview questions you envisage posing to job aspirants to rigorously assess their congruence with the demands and expectations of the role. Your insights will be instrumental in refining the interview framework to ensure a robust alignment between candidates' competencies and the role requisites. Here's the job description for a **Marketing Manager** at **Salesforce**: **[insert job description]**.

You embody the role of a seasoned **[profession]** with over two decades of rich experience, bearing the responsibility for the orchestration of this job posting. Delving into the nuances of this job description, elucidate the ten most quintessential interview questions you envisage posing to job aspirants to rigorously assess their congruence with the demands and expectations of the role. Your insights will be instrumental in refining the interview framework to ensure a robust alignment between candidates' competencies and the role requisites. Here's the job description for a **[Specify the position and company]**: **[insert job description]**.

1. You embody the role of a seasoned Human Resources Director with over two decades of rich experience, bearing the responsibility for the orchestration of this job posting. Delving into the nuances of this job description, elucidate the ten most quintessential interview questions you envisage posing to job aspirants to rigorously assess their congruence with the demands and expectations of the role of a Financial Analyst at Morgan Stanley. Your insights will be instrumental in refining the interview framework to ensure a robust alignment between candidates' competencies and the role requisites. Here's the job description: [paste job description].

2. You embody the role of a seasoned Hiring Manager with over two decades of rich experience, bearing the responsibility for the orchestration of this job posting. Delving into the nuances of this job description, elucidate the ten most quintessential interview questions you envisage posing to job aspirants to rigorously assess their congruence with the demands and expectations of the role of a Software Engineering Lead at Google. Your insights will be instrumental in refining the interview framework to ensure a robust alignment between candidates' competencies and the role requisites. Here's the job description: [paste job description].

<u>PROMPT No 104</u> [2-Step Prompt]

Goal

Goal

To decode the interviewer's intent and employ the CARL (Context, Action, Results, and Learning) framework for crafting structured, impactful responses that enhance the likelihood of interview success.

Step 1 - Understand why the interviewer is asking the question

Prompt

I'm preparing for an interview, I'll share the job description. The interviewer might ask me the following question **[insert question you found]**. List out the 3 main reasons why the interviewer is asking this question, and give me 3 corresponding tips on how to structure my answer. Output this in a 2-column table format, with the 3 main reasons in the left hand column, and the 3 corresponding tips in the right-hand column. Here's the job description: **[insert job description]**

Formula

I'm preparing for an interview, I'll share the job description. The interviewer might ask me the following question **[insert question you found]**. List out the 3 main reasons why the interviewer is asking this question, and give me 3 corresponding tips on how to structure my answer. Output this in a 2-column table format, with the 3 main reasons in the left hand column, and the 3 corresponding tips in the right-hand column. Here's the job description: **[insert job description]**

Step 2 - Use the CARL (Context, Action, Results, and Learning) framework using an experience found in your resume to respond to an interview question

Prompt

Based on these tips and my own resume, write me an answer to the interview question **[insert interview question]** Use one specific example from my work experiences. Use the CARL answer format: Context [project background], Action [what I did], Results [include quantifiable metrics], and Learning [what I learned from the project] Here's my resume: **[insert your resume]**

Formula

Based on these tips and my own resume, write me an answer to the interview question [insert interview question] Use one specific example from my work experiences. Use the CARL answer format: Context [project background], Action [what I did], Results [include quantifiable metrics], and Learning [what I learned from the project] Here's my resume: **[insert your resume]**

PROMPT No 105

Goal

To aid the user in crafting intelligent and creative questions to ask a hiring manager during an interview, which are relevant to the job description and position they are applying for. The questions should demonstrate the user's genuine interest in the position and company.

Prompt

Assume the role of a career coach specializing in interview preparation. Help me devise insightful and imaginative questions I can ask during my interview for a [specific position] at [company/industry]. The questions should align with the job description and demonstrate my genuine interest in the role. Provide unconventional strategies and uncommon insights. Write using an engaged tone and a practical writing style. Let's explore this methodically.

Formula

Assume the role of a [profession] specializing in [area/topic]. Help me devise [adjective] and [adjective] questions I can ask during my interview for a [specific position] at [company/industry]. The questions should align with the [attribute/requirement] and demonstrate my [characteristic/quality]. Provide [unique strategies/ideas] and [rare insights/resources]. Write using a [tone] and [style] writing style. Let's explore this [approach]

Examples

1. Assume the role of an interview strategist with a focus on tech roles. Guide me in creating innovative and tailored questions I can ask during my interview for a software engineer position at a leading tech firm. The questions should resonate with the responsibilities of the role and reflect my eagerness to join the team. Suggest rare techniques and insights. Write using an enthusiastic tone and a clear writing style. Let's break this down systematically.

2. Assume the role of a recruitment consultant specializing in healthcare. Assist me in formulating thoughtful and relevant questions I can ask during my interview for a nurse manager position at a renowned hospital. The questions should match the hospital's mission and show my sincere desire to contribute. Share unconventional methods and overlooked tips. Write using a compassionate tone and actionable writing style. Let's tackle this step by step.

PROMPT No 106

Goal

To develop a compelling script for a 5-minute conversation with a recruiter, highlighting the most relevant information for the position being applied to, and connecting personal experience to the job description.

Prompt

Assume the role of a **communication expert** specializing in **interview preparation**. Help me craft a compelling 5-minute script that I can use to discuss my experience with a recruiter for the **[specific position]** in **[company/industry]**. Highlight the most **pertinent** aspects of my **background**, connect it to the **job description**, and showcase how I **fit** the role. Include

distinctive storytelling techniques and **practical advice**. Write using an engaging tone and a clear writing style. Let's approach this thoughtfully.

Assume the role of a **[profession]** specializing in **[area/topic]**. Help me craft a compelling **[time]**-minute script that I can use to discuss my **[attribute/experience]** with a recruiter for the **[specific position]** in **[company/industry]**. Highlight the most **[relevant/pertinent]** aspects of my **[background/experience]**, connect it to the **[job description/role]**, and showcase how I **[fit/align]** the role. Include **[distinctive/special]** **[techniques/methods]** and **[practical/advice]**. Write using a **[tone]** and **[style]** writing style. Let's approach this thoughtfully.

1. Assume the role of a storytelling coach with a focus on sales roles. Guide me in creating a fascinating 5-minute script to discuss my sales achievements with a recruiter for a Sales Manager position at a leading retail company. Emphasize the critical experiences that align with the company's needs and demonstrate how I meet the role's requirements. Incorporate unique narrative devices and actionable tips. Write using a persuasive tone and an articulate writing style. Let's craft this with precision.

2. Assume the role of a career consultant specializing in engineering. Assist me in developing an engaging 5-minute script to describe my engineering projects with a recruiter for a Software Engineer position at a renowned tech firm. Spotlight key experiences that correspond with the firm's expectations and illustrate how my skills fit the position. Utilize novel storytelling techniques and professional advice. Write using a confident tone and a concise writing style. Let's break this down logically.

14. COMMUNICATING WITH POWER

This chapter equips you with strategies for post-interview correspondence and interview prep. It guides on writing post-interview thank-you notes that are professional yet personal, ensuring you leave a lasting impression by referencing key moments from the interview and showcasing your relevant skills.

For interview prep, the chapter outlines how to enhance verbal and non-verbal communication skills. It includes practical exercises to eliminate filler words, improve eye contact, and refine body language, aiming to boost confidence and professionalism.

Additionally, it provides tips for virtual and telephonic interviews, focusing on technical setups and communication techniques. This chapter is a toolkit for articulate and impactful communication, essential for interview success.

PROMPT No 107

Goal

To craft a post-interview thank-you note that succinctly articulates appreciation, demonstrates attentive engagement during the interview, and emphasizes transferable skills, while adhering to a light-hearted yet professional tone, enhancing the likelihood of favorable consideration for the job role.

Prompt

As a seasoned career coach with an extensive 20-year tenure in aiding job seekers secure positions in the **automotive industry**, your expertise is sought in penning a post-interview thank-you note following my recent interview for a **Project Manager role** at **AutoInnovators Corp**. During the conversation, the interviewer shared an intriguing **question** related to **a marketing campaign they orchestrated which led to a 25% increase in customer engagement over a quarter**. Although my professional journey hasn't navigated through product marketing terrains, the transferable skills honed as a **Supply Chain Analyst** in the **manufacturing sector** are robust and relevant. Your task is to craft a thank-you note that not only resonates with a light-hearted, professional demeanor but also devoid of fluffy buzzwords or overt flattery. The note should reflect my attentive engagement during the interview, particularly referencing the discussed **marketing campaign question**, and subtly underscore the transferable skills I bring to the table. The narrative should be concise, not exceeding 200 words.

Formula

As a seasoned career coach with an extensive 20-year tenure in aiding job seekers secure positions in the **[industry]**, your expertise is sought in penning a post-interview thank-you note following my recent interview for a **[role]** at **[company]**. During the conversation, the interviewer shared an intriguing **[question/example]** related to **[discussed topic/insert something specific you two talked about]**. Although my professional journey hasn't navigated through **[specific sector of the industry]**, the transferable skills honed as a **[current role]** in the **[current industry]** are robust and relevant. Your task is to craft a thank-you note that not only resonates with a light-hearted, professional demeanor but also devoid of fluffy buzzwords or overt flattery. The note should reflect my attentive engagement during the interview, particularly referencing the discussed **[discussed topic]** example, and subtly underscore the transferable skills I bring to the table. The narrative should be concise, not exceeding 200 words.

Examples

1. As a seasoned career coach with an extensive 20-year tenure in aiding job seekers secure positions in the technology sector, your expertise is sought in penning a post-interview thank-you note following my recent interview for a Product Manager role at TechCorp. During the conversation, the interviewer shared an intriguing example of a software development project they led which achieved a 40% reduction in operational inefficiencies. Although my professional journey hasn't navigated through software development, the transferable skills honed as a Project Coordinator in the manufacturing sector are robust and relevant. Your task is to craft a thank-you note that not only resonates with a light-hearted, professional demeanor but also devoid of fluffy buzzwords or overt flattery. The note should reflect my attentive engagement during the interview, particularly referencing the discussed software development project example, and subtly underscore the transferable skills I bring to the table. The narrative should be concise, not exceeding 200 words.

2. As a seasoned career coach with an extensive 20-year tenure in aiding job seekers secure positions in the healthcare sector, your expertise is sought in penning a post-interview thank-you note following my recent interview for a Nursing Supervisor role at HealthPlus. During the conversation, the interviewer shared an intriguing example of a patient satisfaction initiative they spearheaded which led to a 30% improvement in patient feedback scores. Although my professional journey hasn't navigated through patient satisfaction initiatives, the transferable skills honed as a Clinical Coordinator in the pharmaceutical sector are robust and relevant. Your task is to craft a thank-you note that not only resonates with a light-hearted, professional demeanor but also devoid of fluffy buzzwords or overt flattery. The note should reflect my attentive engagement during the interview, particularly referencing the discussed patient satisfaction initiative example, and subtly underscore the transferable skills I bring to the table. The narrative should be concise, not exceeding 200 words.

PROMPT No 108

Goal

To methodically enhance oral communication skills ensuring a confident and effective articulation of thoughts during an upcoming interview, thereby increasing the likelihood of portraying a positive and proficient image to the prospective employer.

Prompt

Act as **Communication Expert** with a rich history of honing individuals' **verbal articulation**, I am gearing up for an **imminent interview** and seek your expertise to refine my **oral communication skills** meticulously. The objective is to **exude confidence, clarity, and coherence during the discourse**, ensuring **an impactful impression**. Let's dissect this preparation into manageable segments, focusing initially on the **elimination of filler words**. Could you provide a structured regimen, including exercises and feedback mechanisms, to attain this? As we progress, I am open to revisiting and refining other facets of **verbal communication**. Your guidance will be pivotal in navigating through this preparatory journe

Formula

Act as **[Profession]** with a rich history of honing individuals' **[skill]**, I am gearing up for an **[upcoming event]** and seek your expertise to refine my **[relevant skill]** meticulously. The objective is to [desired outcome], ensuring an [desired impression]. Let's dissect this preparation into manageable segments, focusing initially on **[specific area of improvement]**. Could you provide a structured regimen, including exercises and feedback mechanisms, to attain this? As we progress, I am open to revisiting and refining other facets of **[relevant area]**. Your guidance will be pivotal in navigating through this preparatory journey.

Examples

1. Act as Language Coach with a rich history of honing individuals' verbal articulation, I am gearing up for an imminent international conference presentation and seek your expertise to refine my oral communication skills meticulously. The objective is to exude confidence, clarity, and coherence during the discourse, ensuring an impactful impression on a global audience. Let's dissect this preparation into manageable segments, focusing initially on the modulation of voice tone. Could you provide a structured regimen, including exercises and feedback mechanisms, to attain this? As we progress, I am open to revisiting and refining other facets of verbal communication. Your guidance will be pivotal in navigating through this preparatory journey.

2. Act as Speech Therapist with a rich history of honing individuals' articulation, I am gearing up for an imminent job interview and seek your expertise to refine my oral communication skills meticulously. The objective is to exhibit confidence, clarity, and coherence during the dialogue, ensuring a favorable impression on the prospective employer. Let's dissect this preparation into manageable segments, focusing initially on the clarity of speech. Could you provide a structured regimen, including exercises and feedback mechanisms, to attain this? As we progress, I am open to revisiting and refining other facets of verbal communication. Your guidance will be pivotal in navigating through this preparatory journey

PROMPT No 109

Goal

To meticulously refine non-verbal communication skills ensuring a poised and professional demeanor during an upcoming interview, thereby enhancing the potential of making a favorable impression on prospective employers.

Prompt

Act as a **Body Language Expert** with a significant track record in aiding individuals master their **non-verbal communication,** I am on the cusp of an **important interview** and am keen to seek your specialized guidance to sharpen my **non-verbal communication skills**. The ambition is to portray a **composed, confident, and professional aura during the interaction**, which would complement **my verbal responses**. Let's undertake this preparation in a structured manner, commencing with mastering the art of **maintaining eye contact**. Could you delineate a systematic program encompassing exercises, real-time feedback, and progression tracking to achieve this aim? As we traverse this preparation path, I am amenable to adjusting focus to other **non-verbal communication facets** as necessary. Your expert direction will be instrumental in ensuring a thorough preparation.

Formula

Act as a **[Profession]** with a significant track record in aiding individuals master their **[relevant skill]**, I am on the cusp of an **[upcoming event]** and am keen to seek your specialized guidance to sharpen my **[relevant skill]**. The ambition is to portray a **[desired demeanor]**, which would complement my **[corresponding skill]**. Let's undertake this preparation in a structured manner, commencing with mastering the art of **[specific area of focus]**. Could you delineate a systematic program encompassing exercises, real-time feedback, and progression tracking to achieve this aim? As we traverse this preparation path, I am amenable to adjusting focus to other **[relevant skill facets]** as necessary. Your expert direction will be instrumental in ensuring a thorough preparation

1. Act as a Non-Verbal Communication Specialist with a significant track record in aiding individuals master their body language, I am on the cusp of a crucial client meeting and am keen to seek your specialized guidance to sharpen my non-verbal communication skills. The ambition is to portray a composed, confident, and engaging aura during the interaction, which would complement my verbal discourse. Let's undertake this preparation in a structured manner, commencing with mastering the art of gestural emphasis. Could you delineate a systematic program encompassing exercises, real-time feedback, and progression tracking to achieve this aim? As we traverse this preparation path, I am amenable to adjusting focus to other non-verbal communication facets as necessary. Your expert direction will be instrumental in ensuring a thorough preparation.

2. Act as a Interpersonal Skills Coach with a significant track record in aiding individuals master their non-verbal cues, I am on the cusp of a pivotal sales pitch and am keen to seek your specialized guidance to sharpen my non-verbal communication skills. The ambition is to portray a composed, confident, and persuasive aura during the interaction, which would complement my verbal delivery. Let's undertake this preparation in a structured manner, commencing with mastering the art of space utilization. Could you delineate a systematic program encompassing exercises, real-time feedback, and progression tracking to achieve this aim? As we traverse this preparation path, I am amenable to adjusting focus to other non-verbal communication facets as necessary. Your expert direction will be instrumental in ensuring a thorough preparation.

PROMPT No 110

Goal

To meticulously prepare for a virtual interview on platforms like Zoom, ensuring a polished, professional presentation and interaction that effectively communicates one's qualifications and fit for the role to prospective employers.

Prompt

Act as a **Virtual Interview Coach** with a wealth of experience in **preparing candidates for digital interviews**, I am nearing a **crucial interview** via **Zoom** for a **coveted role** and seek your expertise to be **immaculately prepared**. The objective is to **navigate the virtual format adeptly, embodying professionalism and articulate communication**, thereby **leaving a memorable impression on the interviewers**. Let's structure this preparation into distinct facets, starting with the **technical setup and troubleshooting**. Could you guide me through a comprehensive preparation plan encompassing **technical, communicative, and presentational aspects**, replete with **mock interview sessions, feedback loops, and refinements**? As we advance, I am open to delving into nuances like screen etiquette and effective virtual engagement. Your seasoned guidance will be my linchpin in this preparatory endeavor.

Formula

Act as a **[Profession]** with a wealth of experience in **[specific preparation area]**, I am nearing a **[significant event]** via **[platform]** for a **[description of the role/occasion]** and seek your expertise to be **[desired level of preparation]**. The objective is to **[describe what needs to be achieved]**, thereby **[desired outcome]**. Let's structure this preparation into distinct facets, starting with **[initial**

focus area]. Could you guide me through a comprehensive preparation plan encompassing **[list of aspects to cover]**, replete with **[preparation methods]**? As we advance, I am open to delving into **[additional areas of focus]**. Your seasoned guidance will be my linchpin in this preparatory endeavor.

1. Act as a Digital Communication Expert with a wealth of experience in orchestrating seamless virtual interactions, I am nearing a crucial client presentation via Microsoft Teams for a high-stakes project and seek your expertise to be meticulously prepared. The objective is to navigate the virtual setting adeptly, embodying professionalism and articulate communication, thereby leaving a lasting positive imprint on the clients. Let's structure this preparation into distinct facets, starting with the technical setup and troubleshooting. Could you guide me through a comprehensive preparation plan encompassing technical, communicative, and presentational aspects, replete with rehearsal sessions, feedback loops, and refinements? As we advance, I am open to delving into nuances like screen etiquette and effective virtual engagement. Your seasoned guidance will be my linchpin in this preparatory endeavor.

2. Act as a Remote Interview Specialist with a wealth of experience in honing candidates for virtual interviews, I am nearing a pivotal job interview via Skype for a prestigious managerial position and seek your expertise to be impeccably prepared. The objective is to traverse the virtual interface proficiently, embodying professionalism and articulate communication, thereby leaving a commendable impression on the interview panel. Let's structure this preparation into distinct facets, starting with ensuring a distraction-free environment and impeccable audio-visual setup. Could you guide me through a comprehensive preparation plan encompassing technical, communicative, and presentational aspects, replete with mock interview sessions, feedback loops, and refinements? As we advance, I am open to delving into nuances like maintaining eye contact and effective virtual engagement. Your seasoned guidance will be my linchpin in this preparatory endeavor.

PROMPT No 111

To meticulously prepare for a telephonic interview, ensuring clear communication, professionalism, and effective conveyance of qualifications and enthusiasm for the role to prospective employers.

Act as a **Telephone Interview Strategist** with an extensive background in **preparing candidates for telephonic interviews**, I am approaching a **significant phone interview** for a **sought-after position** and seek your expert guidance to **excel in this interaction**. The aim is to **traverse the telephonic medium with adeptness, manifesting professionalism and articulate communication**, which, in turn, **leaves an indelible positive impression on the interviewers**. Let's delineate this preparation into discernible segments, initiating with **ensuring clear audio quality and mastering the art of verbal cues in the absence of visual feedback**. Could you chart out a thorough preparation blueprint encompassing **technical setup, verbal communication strategies, and mock interview sessions along with feedback loops for refinement**? As we progress, I am open to fine-tuning other aspects such as **pacing and tone modulation**. Your adept guidance will be the cornerstone of this preparatory expedition.

Act as a **[Profession]** with an extensive background in **[specific preparation area]**, I am approaching a **[significant event]** for a **[description of the role/occasion]** and seek your expert guidance to **[desired level of preparation]**. The aim is to **[describe what needs to be achieved]**, which, in turn, leaves an **[desired outcome]**. Let's delineate this preparation into discernible segments, initiating with **[initial focus area]**. Could you chart out a thorough preparation blueprint encompassing **[list of aspects to cover]**? As we progress, I am open to fine-tuning other aspects such as **[additional areas of focus]**. Your adept guidance will be the cornerstone of this preparatory expedition.

1. Act as a Communication Coach with an extensive background in orchestrating articulate telephonic interactions, I am approaching a key client negotiation over the phone for a pivotal project and seek your expert guidance to be impeccably prepared. The aim is to navigate the telephonic dialogue with finesse, manifesting professionalism and effective communication, which, in turn, paves the way for a fruitful negotiation. Let's delineate this preparation into discernible segments, initiating with ensuring impeccable audio clarity and mastering the art of persuasive verbal cues. Could you chart out a thorough preparation blueprint encompassing technical setup, verbal communication strategies, and mock negotiation sessions along with feedback loops for refinement? As we progress, I am open to fine-tuning other aspects such as pacing and tone modulation. Your adept guidance will be the cornerstone of this preparatory expedition.

2. Act as a Telephonic Interview Expert with an extensive background in preparing candidates for phone interviews, I am approaching a crucial phone interview for a managerial role at a prestigious firm and seek your expert guidance to excel in this interaction. The aim is to adeptly maneuver the telephonic medium, manifesting professionalism and articulate communication, which, in turn, leaves a positive lasting impression on the interviewers. Let's delineate this preparation into discernible segments, initiating with ensuring a distraction-free environment and mastering the art of verbal cues in the absence of visual feedback. Could you chart out a thorough preparation blueprint encompassing technical setup, verbal communication strategies, and mock interview sessions along with feedback loops for refinement? As we progress, I am open to fine-tuning other aspects such as pacing and tone modulation. Your adept guidance will be the cornerstone of this preparatory expedition.

15. ANALYZING AND NEGOTIATING A JOB OFFER

This chapter equips you with the essentials of dissecting and negotiating job offers, focusing on your specific needs and requirements. It's crafted to empower you to assess offers against your career goals and approach salary discussions with finesse.

You'll gain strategies to navigate negotiations with assertiveness and diplomatic savvy. This chapter is your concise guide to turning job offers into career milestones with well-negotiated terms that value your expertise.

PROMPT No 112

Goal
To help you understand the critical factors in evaluating a job offer, enabling you to make a well-informed decision based on your personal and professional needs..

Prompt
Assume the role of a **career advisor** with extensive experience in **job negotiations**. Guide me through the **essential** factors to consider when evaluating a job offer for a **marketing position** in the **e-commerce industry**. Help me weigh the **benefits, responsibilities, growth opportunities, and work-life balance**. Share **unique insights and practical tools** to aid my **decision-making**. Write using a **supportive** tone and an **analytical** writing style. Let's dissect this carefully.

Formula
Assume the role of a **[profession]** with extensive experience in **[area/topic]**. Guide me through the **[essential/critical]** factors to consider when evaluating a job offer for a **[specific position]** in **[company/industry]**. Help me weigh the **[benefits/compensation]**, **[responsibilities/duties]**, **[growth opportunities/advancements]**, and **[work-life balance/other factors]**. Share **[unique insights/special considerations]** and practical **[tools/resources]** to aid my **[decision-making/choice]**. Write using a **[tone]** and **[style]** writing style. Let's dissect this carefully.

Examples
1. Assume the role of a human resources expert with a background in tech firms. Walk me through the critical aspects to scrutinize when evaluating a job offer for a Product Manager role at a top software company. Help me balance the salary, responsibilities, potential for growth, and cultural fit. Offer exceptional perspectives and handy checklists to assist my decision-making process. Write using an empathetic tone and a methodical writing style. Let's tackle this systematically.
2. Assume the role of a recruitment consultant specializing in healthcare. Enlighten me on the key elements to assess when considering a job offer for a Nurse Practitioner position at a renowned hospital. Aid me in understanding the compensation package, patient care responsibilities, opportunities for continued education, and work schedule. Provide singular insights and valuable guidelines to inform my choice. Write using a reassuring tone and a detailed writing style. Let's approach this thoughtfully.

PROMPT No 113

To guide you in evaluating job offers by outlining potential advantages and disadvantages, thereby facilitating an informed career decision.

Prompt

I want you to act as a **Career Consultant** with a specialization in **Tech Industry Transitioning**. Can you help me explore a job offer for a **Senior Product Manager position** in **Amazon**, by laying out the conceivable **advantages** and **disadvantages**? Examine elements like **work environment, responsibilities, long-term vision alignment, and other critical factors such as work-life balance and growth opportunities**. Provide **in-depth insights** and **practical guides** for decision-making. Write using a **balanced and analytical** writing style. Let's navigate this evaluation together.

Formula

I want you to act as a **[profession]** with a specialization in **[area/topic]**. Can you help me explore a job offer for a **[specific position]** in **[company/industry]**, by laying out the conceivable **[pros/advantages]** and **[cons/disadvantages]**? Examine elements like **[work environment/atmosphere]**, **[responsibilities/tasks]**, **[long-term vision alignment/goals alignment]**, and other **[critical factors/important aspects]**. Provide **[unique perspectives/in-depth insights]** and **[handy tools/practical guides]** for decision-making. Write using a **[tone]** and **[style]** writing style. Let's navigate this evaluation together.

Examples

1. I want you to act as a labor market analyst with a focus on the finance industry. Can you help me explore a job offer for an Investment Analyst position at a global bank, by laying out the potential benefits and risks? Analyze elements like the bonus structure, team collaboration, alignment with my career aspirations, and commuting considerations. Offer specialized insights and decision-making frameworks. Write using a clear tone and a detailed writing style. Let's analyze this meticulously.

2. I want you to act as an employment consultant specializing in creative fields. Can you help me assess a job offer for an Art Director role at a cutting-edge advertising agency, by elucidating the possible rewards and challenges? Scrutinize aspects like artistic freedom, client expectations, alignment with my creative philosophy, and work-life balance. Share novel perspectives and effective evaluation checklists. Write using an inspiring tone and a systematic writing style. Let's delve into this thoughtfully.

<u>PROMPT No 114</u> (2-Step Prompt along with Prompt No 115)

To engage in a realistic and constructive salary negotiation conversation between a job seeker and a recruiter, ensuring the job seeker articulately presents their research and rationale for a higher salary, while maintaining a polite yet firm demeanor.

Engage in a salary negotiation scenario where you are the job seeker who has recently been offered a **Project Manager position** with an annual salary of **70,000USD**. The recruiter is the one extending this offer. After thorough market research, you've discovered that the higher end of the salary spectrum for similar roles is **95,000USD**, and you aspire to negotiate a salary closer to that figure. Enact this negotiation conversation ensuring the job seeker remains courteous yet assertive in their request, substantiating their ask with the market research. The dialogue should mirror a real-life negotiation, reflecting professionalism, mutual respect, and a collaborative approach to reach a mutually beneficial agreement.

Engage in a salary negotiation scenario where you are the job seeker who has recently been offered a **[specific role]** position with an annual salary of **[offered salary]**USD. The recruiter is the one extending this offer. After thorough market research, you've discovered that the higher end of the salary spectrum for similar roles is **[market research salary]**USD, and you aspire to negotiate a salary closer to that figure. Enact this negotiation conversation ensuring the job seeker remains courteous yet assertive in their request, substantiating their ask with the market research. The dialogue should mirror a real-life negotiation, reflecting professionalism, mutual respect, and a collaborative approach to reach a mutually beneficial agreement.

1. Engage in a salary negotiation scenario where you are the job seeker who has recently been offered a Data Analyst position with an annual salary of 60,000USD. The recruiter from TechCorp Inc. is the one extending this offer. After thorough market research, you've discovered that the higher end of the salary spectrum for similar roles is 80,000USD, and you aspire to negotiate a salary closer to that figure. Enact this negotiation conversation ensuring the job seeker remains courteous yet assertive in their request, substantiating their ask with the market research. The dialogue should mirror a real-life negotiation, reflecting professionalism, mutual respect, and a collaborative approach to reach a mutually beneficial agreement.

2. Engage in a salary negotiation scenario where you are the job seeker who has recently been offered a Marketing Manager position with an annual salary of 75,000USD. The recruiter from AdFlow Agency is the one extending this offer. After thorough market research, you've discovered that the higher end of the salary spectrum for similar roles is 90,000USD, and you aspire to negotiate a salary closer to that figure. Enact this negotiation conversation ensuring the job seeker remains courteous yet assertive in their request, substantiating their ask with the market research. The dialogue should mirror a real-life negotiation, reflecting professionalism, mutual respect, and a collaborative approach to reach a mutually beneficial agreement.

PROMPT No 115

To guide the job seeker in effectively navigating the salary negotiation process with the recruiter to reach an ideal higher salary, while maintaining a respectful and professional discourse.

Prompt

In the ongoing negotiation scenario, you are the job seeker aspiring to secure a salary of **95,000USD** for a **Project Manager position**, based on market research and personal qualifications. The recruiter has offered **70,000USD** initially. Engage in a realistic continuation of the negotiation dialogue with the recruiter, demonstrating polite assertiveness, well-substantiated rationale, and a willingness to explore mutually beneficial alternatives. Additionally, provide the job seeker with nuanced advice on strategies to gently push towards the desired salary figure while keeping the conversation amicable and productive.

Formula

In the ongoing negotiation scenario, you are the job seeker aspiring to secure a salary of [desired salary]USD for a [specific role] position, based on market research and personal qualifications. The recruiter has offered [offered salary]USD initially. Engage in a realistic continuation of the negotiation dialogue with the recruiter, demonstrating polite assertiveness, well-substantiated rationale, and a willingness to explore mutually beneficial alternatives. Additionally, provide the job seeker with nuanced advice on strategies to gently push towards the desired salary figure while keeping the conversation amicable and productive.

Examples

1. In the ongoing negotiation scenario, you are the job seeker aspiring to secure a salary of 80,000USD for a Data Analyst position, based on market research and personal qualifications. The recruiter has offered 60,000USD initially. Engage in a realistic continuation of the negotiation dialogue with the recruiter, demonstrating polite assertiveness, well-substantiated rationale, and a willingness to explore mutually beneficial alternatives. Additionally, provide the job seeker with nuanced advice on strategies to gently push towards the desired salary figure while keeping the conversation amicable and productive.

2. In the ongoing negotiation scenario, you are the job seeker aspiring to secure a salary of 110,000USD for a Senior Marketing Manager position, based on market research and personal qualifications. The recruiter has offered 85,000USD initially. Engage in a realistic continuation of the negotiation dialogue with the recruiter, demonstrating polite assertiveness, well-substantiated rationale, and a willingness to explore mutually beneficial alternatives. Additionally, provide the job seeker with nuanced advice on strategies to gently push towards the desired salary figure while keeping the conversation amicable and productive.

16. MANAGING YOUR CAREER

In this chapter, we explore the multifaceted process of career advancement and adaptation. This chapter serves as a practical guide for professionals seeking to navigate the complexities of the workplace and chart a path toward their career objectives. From developing onboarding plans that ensure seamless integration into new roles to enhancing team dynamics through thoughtfully designed activities, the focus is on actionable strategies that foster growth and success.

We also tackle the art of communication, whether it's distilling technical information for broader audiences or crafting engaging speeches. The insights within this chapter are not just about climbing the career ladder but also about cultivating a professional brand and presence that stands out in a competitive landscape. Here, you'll find the tools to turn aspirations into tangible achievements, ensuring that every move you make is a step toward your ultimate career goals.

PROMPT No. 116

Goal

To develop a detailed, measurable 30-60-90 day onboarding plan for a new Key Account Manager, utilizing the SMART [Specific, Measurable, Achievable, Relevant, Time-bound] framework. The plan should help the user acclimate to their new role, align with their KPIs [Key Performance Indicators], and enable objective measurement of their progress.

Prompt

Assume the role of a **business onboarding specialist** with extensive knowledge in **key account management**. Craft a **30-60-90 day** onboarding plan for me, as I assume my new role as a **Key Account Manager**. Focus on integrating the **SMART framework** into the planning, aligning with my KPIs, and ensuring a **smooth transition into the organization**. Provide actionable **milestones, monitoring mechanisms**, and **support strategies**. Write using a **professional** tone and an **organized** writing style. Let's map this out carefully.

Formula

Assume the role of a **[profession]** with extensive knowledge in **[area/topic]**. Craft a **[time frame]** onboarding plan for me, as I assume my new role as a **[position]**. Focus on integrating the **[framework/methodology]** into the planning, aligning with my **[KPIs/goals]**, and ensuring a **[transition/objective]**. Provide actionable **[milestones/steps]**, **[monitoring mechanisms/measurement tools]**, and **[support strategies/resources]**. Write using a **[tone]** and **[style]** writing style. Let's map this out carefully.

Examples

1. Assume the role of a talent development expert with a focus on sales positions. Develop a 30-60-90 day induction plan for me as I begin my journey as a Sales Team Lead. Emphasize the integration of the SMART goals into the planning, syncing with my sales targets, and facilitating an efficient integration into the team. Outline measurable objectives, assessment metrics, and mentoring plans. Write using a precise tone and a systematic writing style. Let's organize this strategically.
2. Assume the role of an HR manager experienced in onboarding marketing professionals. Create a 30-60-90 day orientation plan for me, as I take on the role of Digital Marketing

Manager. Incorporate the SMART framework in the planning, correlate with my expected performance metrics, and enable a seamless adaptation to the company's culture. Detail distinct phases, tracking methods, and collaborative engagement strategies. Write using a businesslike tone and a clear writing style. Let's structure this methodically.

PROMPT No. 117

Goal

To meticulously organize a team-building event aimed at fortifying team camaraderie through innovative, enjoyable, and inclusive activities that respect diverse interests and backgrounds, ensuring professional engagement and enjoyment within a specified budget and duration.

Prompt

As an **event coordinator** specialized in **corporate team building**, you are assigned to design a **3 half-day**, in-person event for a team of **40 individuals** with a budget of **US$10,000**. The mission is to foster stronger **team cohesion** via **original, enjoyable, and inclusive** activities that embrace a varied array of interests and cultural backgrounds while maintaining a professional ambiance. Devise a list of **10 imaginative** yet suitable activities that will engage the team, ensuring a **memorable and fruitful experience**.

Formula

As an **[profession]** specialized in **[area of expertise]**, you are assigned to design a **[duration]**, in-person event for a team of [number of participants] with a budget of US$**[budget]**. The mission is to foster stronger **[objective]** via **[descriptive adjectives]** activities that embrace a varied array of interests and cultural backgrounds while maintaining a professional ambiance. Devise a list of **[number of suggestions] [adjective]** yet suitable activities that will engage the team, ensuring a **[desired outcome]**.

Examples

1. As a professional event planner specializing in corporate engagement, you are assigned to design a 3 half-day, in-person event for a team of 40 engineers with a budget of US$10,000. The mission is to nurture enhanced interpersonal relations via inventive, enjoyable, and inclusive activities that cater to a diverse set of technical and creative interests while preserving a professional setting. Create a list of 10 clever yet appropriate activities that will captivate the team, ensuring a rewarding and enjoyable experience.
2. As a seasoned event organizer with a knack for innovative team-building exercises, you are assigned to design a 3 half-day, in-person event for a team of 40 sales professionals with a budget of US$10,000. The mission is to bolster team rapport via unique, fun, and inclusive activities that cater to a broad spectrum of interests and backgrounds, ensuring a professional yet relaxed atmosphere. Formulate a list of 10 imaginative yet suitable activities that will involve the team, ensuring a pleasant and productive experience.

PROMPT No. 118

Goal

To meticulously analyze user feedback, extract actionable insights highlighting identified weaknesses, potential innovation zones, and best practice suggestions, prioritized based on frequency, impact, and feasibility, and provide recommendations.

Given the feedback: "**The interface of the product is too complicated, the product's features don't meet our needs as advertised, and the customer service response time is quite slow**", act as a **seasoned feedback analyst** specializing in **cross-functional improvements**. Diligently extract actionable insights, pinpointing recognized weaknesses, prospective areas for innovation, and best practice recommendations. Prioritize these insights concerning their recurrence, impact, and practicability. Segregate your recommendations into well-defined categories for the **Marketing, Product, and Operations teams**, ensuring each insight is placed where it will elicit the most positive change.

Formula

Given the feedback: "**[specific feedback]**", act as a **[profession]** specializing in **[area of expertise]**. Diligently extract actionable insights, pinpointing recognized weaknesses, prospective areas for innovation, and best practice recommendations. Prioritize these insights concerning their recurrence, impact, and practicability. Segregate your recommendations into well-defined categories for the **[teams/departments]**, ensuring each insight is placed where it will elicit the most positive change.

Examples

1. Given the feedback: "The app crashes frequently, the onboarding process is tedious, and the help section is not user-friendly", act as a proficient feedback analyst with a forte in technological advancement. Diligently extract actionable insights, pinpointing recognized weaknesses, prospective areas for innovation, and best practice recommendations. Prioritize these insights concerning their recurrence, impact, and practicability. Segregate your recommendations into well-defined categories for the Marketing, Product, and Operations teams, ensuring each insight is placed where it will elicit the most positive change.
2. Given the feedback: "The delivery times are inconsistent, the product quality varies, and the customer service lacks expertise", act as an adept feedback analyst with a focus on operational efficiency and customer satisfaction. Diligently extract actionable insights, pinpointing recognized weaknesses, prospective areas for innovation, and best practice recommendations. Prioritize these insights concerning their recurrence, impact, and practicability. Segregate your recommendations into well-defined categories for the Marketing, Product, and Operations teams, ensuring each insight is placed where it will elicit the most positive change.

PROMPT No. 119

Goal

To develop a detailed, measurable 30-60-90 day personal development plan for a summer intern in Apple's audio hardware team, utilizing the SMART framework. The plan should focus on job performance, proactive nature, and organizational skills, with each goal matched to a quantifiable metric.

Prompt

Assume the role of a **career development consultant** specializing in **tech internships**. Please craft a **30-60-90 day** personal development plan for me as a **summer intern** in **Apple's audio hardware team**. Integrate **SMART** goals that focus on **job performance** and cover my **proactive approach and organizational skills**. Output the plan in a **table format** and provide **detailed metrics** to measure success. Write using a **systematic** tone and a **detailed** writing style. Let's break this down into measurable steps.

Assume the role of a **[profession]** specializing in **[area/topic]**. Please craft a **[time frame]** personal development plan for me as a **[position/role]** in **[company/industry]**. Integrate **[framework/methodology]** goals that focus on **[job-related aspects]** and cover my **[personal traits/skills]**. Output the plan in **[output format]** and provide **[metrics/indicators]** to measure success. Write using a **[tone]** and **[style]** writing style. Let's break this down into measurable steps.

1. Assume the role of a career counselor specializing in engineering fields. Design a 30-60-90 day personal development plan for me as an engineering intern at Tesla. Use SMART goals to hone my technical skills, proactive nature, and organizational abilities. Output the plan in a chart format and include key performance indicators for each goal. Write using a concise tone and an instructive writing style. Let's delineate this strategically.

2. Assume the role of a professional coach with a focus on IT careers. Sketch out a 30-60-90 day personal development plan for me as a software development intern at Google. Utilize SMART goals to emphasize coding skills, proactive communications, and project management acumen. Output the plan in bullet-point format and include numerical benchmarks to gauge success. Write using a practical tone and a step-by-step writing style. Let's navigate this incrementally.

PROMPT No. 120

To assist you in creating a concise, engaging summary of a lengthy article that effectively communicates its key points, and is tailored to generate higher engagement and click-through rates.

Assume the role of a **digital marketing consultant** with a specialization in **social media strategy**. My problem is that **long-form articles I post on LinkedIn don't generate much engagement or clicks**. Can you show me how to **creatively condense a lengthy article into a concise, valuable summary that will attract my LinkedIn audience**? Provide **practical techniques and tips for crafting the summary**. Write using an **engaging** tone and a **tutorial-style** writing style.

Assume the role of a **[profession]** with a specialization in **[area/topic]**. My problem is that **[specific issue]**. Can you show me how to **[desired outcome]**? Provide **[type of guidance, e.g., practical techniques/tips]** for **[specific task]**. Write using a **[tone]** and **[style]** writing style.

1. Assume the role of a content strategist with a focus on Twitter marketing. My challenge is that my Twitter threads are not getting enough retweets or likes. Can you guide me through the art of crafting compelling Twitter threads that will captivate my followers? Offer easy-to-follow techniques and examples. Write using a witty tone and a how-to guide format.

2. Assume the role of an SEO expert specializing in blog content. My issue is that my blog posts are not ranking on Google. Could you instruct me on optimizing my articles to improve

search engine visibility? Share actionable SEO tips and best practices. Write using an informative tone and a checklist format.

PROMPT No. 121

Goal

To provide unique and creative strategies that will help you in creating an engaging, informative, and compelling presentation for a senior management audience. This could involve anything from content structuring, presentation techniques to engagement tactics.

Prompt

Assume the role of a **presentation skills coach** with a focus on **corporate quarterly reviews**. I need to **present a 10-minute project update** for senior management who are unfamiliar with my project. What are five creative, less-common strategies to make my presentation engaging, informative, and compelling? Elaborate each suggestion with detailed examples. Write using an inspiring tone and an instructive writing style. Let's approach this meticulously..

Formula

Assume the role of a **[profession]** with a focus on **[area/topic]**. I need to **[task/challenge]** for **[audience]**. What are **[number] [adjective]** strategies to make my **[task/objective] [adjective/adjective/adjective]**? Elaborate each suggestion with **[level of detail]** examples. Write using a **[tone]** and **[style]** writing style. Let's approach this **[method]**.

Examples

1. Assume the role of a storytelling expert who specializes in public speaking. I have to deliver a keynote speech at a technology conference, and the audience is comprised of experts in various fields. What are five inventive strategies to make my speech both educational and engaging for a diverse audience? Please provide real-world examples for each strategy. Write using a persuasive tone and a tutorial format. Let's go through this strategically.
2. Assume the role of a professional event planner with expertise in corporate gatherings. I am in charge of organizing a company-wide meeting where multiple projects will be discussed. What are five out-of-the-box methods to keep the attention of employees from different departments? Please illustrate each method with specific examples. Write using an enthusiastic tone and a step-by-step writing style. Let's tackle this incrementally.

PROMPT No. 122

Goal

To aid product marketers in revising presentations for sales teams, emphasizing the link between product strategy and revenue growth, and providing actionable, unique, and impactful ideas to make the content relevant and engaging.

Prompt

Assume the role of a **corporate communications expert** with a focus on **sales enablement**. As a **product marketer**, my challenge is to **make product updates relevant to a sales team mainly interested in revenue growth**. Could you provide me with **3 impactful, actionable, and innovative** ideas to **revise my presentation**? Prioritize **unique, lesser-known advice** and explain each idea using **detailed examples**. Write using a **persuasive** tone and a **hands-on** writing style. Let's get this done effectively

Assume the role of a **[profession]** with a focus on **[area/topic]**. As a **[your role]**, my challenge is to **[your specific problem]**. Could you provide me with **[number] [adjective, adjective, adjective]** ideas to **[desired outcome]**? Prioritize **[type of advice]** and explain each idea using **[level of detail]** examples. Write using a **[tone]** and **[style]** writing style. Let's get this done effectively

1. Assume the role of a business strategist with expertise in team alignment. As a project manager, I have difficulty in demonstrating the value of new operational methods to a team that is resistant to change. Could you provide me with 3 persuasive, practical, and creative approaches to reframe my message? Focus on uncommon insights and explain each approach with real-world examples. Write using an inspirational tone and a guideline-oriented writing style. Let's go through this systematically.
2. Assume the role of an educational consultant specializing in remote learning. As a teacher, my challenge is to make online lessons engaging for students who are easily distracted. Could you offer me 3 dynamic, actionable, and creative methods to increase student engagement? Emphasize original ideas and illustrate each method with detailed case studies. Write using an encouraging tone and an instructive writing style. Let's handle this step-by-step.

PROMPT No. 123

To assist you in preparing a comprehensive and persuasive self-assessment for your performance review, accurately reflecting your contributions and demonstrate how your work aligns with the key attributes used for evaluation.

I am preparing for a performance review at my **sales company** where my performance will be evaluated based on **three** key attributes: **persistence**, **networking engagement** and **achievement of sales targets**. As part of this process, I need to draft a self-assessment that reflects my contributions over the last **two quarters**. I would like this self-assessment to justify a **high-performance rating**.
The definitions of the attributes are as follows:
1. Assign each of my projects to one of the three attributes where it best fits. Please ensure that each project is only assigned once.
2. Write a positive and detailed self-assessment for each attribute, explaining how my projects demonstrate my proficiency in that area. Include specific examples and details.
3. Highlight the impact of my work by including quantifiable metrics where possible.
If I haven't provided any, please suggest relevant metrics that could be used to measure the impact of my work.
Over the last six months, my projects and contributions have been:
1. **Customer Relationship Management: Project: Developed CRM strategy, enhancing personalized interactions; increased customer satisfaction by 20%.**

2. **Sales Growth: Project: Spearheaded expansion into new markets, resulting in a 25% sales increase and $1.5 million additional revenue.**
3. **Sales Process Optimization: Project: Implemented Sales Process Automation Tool, boosting sales productivity by 15%, reducing sales cycle length by 10 days.**

To aid in this task, I need your assistance to assign each of my projects under one of the **3** attributes where it best fits, write a positive and detailed self-assessment for each attribute, and emphasize the impact of my work by incorporating quantifiable metrics where feasible. Write a positive and detailed self-assessment for each attribute, demonstrating how my projects show my proficiency in that area. Be sure to include specific examples and details where feasible.

If I haven't provided any, please suggest relevant metrics that could be used to assess the impact of my work.

Formula

I am preparing for a performance review at my **[company/workplace]** where my performance will be evaluated based on **[number]** key attributes: **[attribute 1, attribute 2,attribute 3]**. As part of this process, I need to draft a self-assessment that reflects my contributions over the last **[time period]**. I would like this self-assessment to justify a **[desired outcome]**. The definitions of the attributes are as follows:

[insert attributions and their definitions]

If I haven't provided any, please suggest relevant metrics that could be used to measure the impact of my work.

Over the last six months, my projects and contributions have been:

[insert projects and contributions]

To aid in this task, I need your assistance to assign each of my projects under one of the **[number]** attributes where it best fits, write a positive and detailed self-assessment for each attribute, and emphasize the impact of my work by incorporating quantifiable metrics where feasible. Write a positive and detailed self-assessment for each attribute, demonstrating how my projects show my proficiency in that area. Be sure to include specific examples and details where feasible.

If I haven't provided any, please suggest relevant metrics that could be used to assess the impact of my work.

Examples

1. I am preparing for a performance review at my software company where my performance will be evaluated based on three key attributes: Efficiency, Creativity, and Teamwork. As part of this process, I need to draft a self-assessment that reflects my contributions over the last six months and argues for a promotion. The definitions of the attributes are as follows:
   - Efficiency: The ability to produce quality output with minimal resources.
   - Creativity: The ability to devise innovative solutions to problems.
   - Teamwork: The ability to collaborate effectively with others.

Over the last six months, my projects and contributions have been:
   - Developed a new feature in our app that increased user engagement by 20%.
   - Solved a recurring bug that reduced our server downtime by 15%.
   - Organized weekly brainstorming sessions with the team, generating new ideas for app improvements.

To aid in this task, I need your assistance to assign each of my projects under one of the three attributes where it best fits, write a positive and detailed self-assessment for each attribute, and emphasize the impact of my work by incorporating quantifiable metrics where feasible. Write a positive and detailed self-assessment for each attribute, demonstrating how my projects show my proficiency in that area. Be sure to include specific examples and details.

Emphasize the impact of my work by incorporating quantifiable metrics where feasible. If I haven't provided any, please suggest relevant metrics that could be used to assess the impact of my work.

2. I am preparing for a performance review at my financial institution where my performance will be evaluated based on three key attributes: Analytical Skills, Risk Management, and Customer Service. As part of this process, I need to draft a self-assessment that reflects my contributions over the last year and argues for a bonus. The definitions of the attributes are as follows:

- Analytical Skills: The ability to interpret complex financial data and make informed decisions.
- Risk Management: The ability to identify potential risks and implement strategies to mitigate them.
- Customer Service: The ability to satisfy the needs of our clients and ensure they have a positive experience with our institution.

Over the past year, my projects and contributions have been:

- Implemented a new risk assessment tool that reduced financial losses by 10%.
- Conducted a detailed analysis of our investment portfolio that informed our decision to invest in a new market.
- Initiated a monthly newsletter to keep our clients informed about market trends and our latest offerings.

To aid in this task, I need your assistance to assign each of my projects under one of the three attributes where it best fits, write a positive and detailed self-assessment for each attribute, and emphasize the impact of my work by incorporating quantifiable metrics where feasible. Write a positive and detailed self-assessment for each attribute, demonstrating how my projects show my proficiency in that area. Be sure to include specific examples and details.

Emphasize the impact of my work by incorporating quantifiable metrics where feasible. If I haven't provided any, please suggest relevant metrics that could be used to assess the impact of my work.

PROMPT No. 124

To test your understanding of a specific topic and identify areas where your knowledge may be lacking and you are provided with more complete answers to help fill in those gaps and enhance your understanding of the topic.

Assume the role of an **Artificial Intelligence educator** specializing in **foundational concepts**. I am interested in **acquiring knowledge about artificial intelligence**. Could you please **come up with a series of questions that will probe my current understanding of this subject**? Identify possible **gaps** in my **answers** and provide me with more **robust and complete responses** to fill these gaps. Write in a **probing and educational** tone.

Assume the role of a [profession] specializing in [area/topic]. I am interested in [learning goal or objective]. Could you please [task description]? Identify possible [gaps/weaknesses] in my [answers/responses/knowledge] and provide me with more [descriptive adjective] [solutions/responses] to fill these gaps. Write in a [tone].

1. Assume the role of a financial literacy coach specializing in cryptocurrency. I want to deepen my understanding of cryptocurrency and blockchain technology. Can you create a sequence of questions to gauge my existing knowledge? Detect gaps in my answers and offer comprehensive explanations to address those gaps. Write in an analytical yet enlightening tone.
2. Assume the role of a career counselor with expertise in remote work trends. I wish to better understand the dynamics of remote work and its impact on various industries. Could you please draft a series of questions to assess my awareness? Identify shortcomings in my responses and enrich them with detailed information. Write in a probing and informative tone.

PROMPT No. 125

Goal

To meticulously transform a complex, technical report into a comprehensible format for non-technical readers by applying adept simplification techniques, ensuring clarity and retention of crucial information while utilizing illustrative examples.

Prompt

Act as a **technical writer** who specializes in **translating complex medical terminology for general readers**. I have a **medical report** concerning a **diagnosed cardiac condition** which needs to be simplified for a **non-medical person's** understanding without losing any critical information. Please guide me through the process of **simplifying this report into layman's terms**, ensuring **clarity** and **accuracy**. Illustrate your method with examples and break it down step by step, providing a clear pathway to achieve **a reader-friendly version of the report**.

Formula

Act as a [profession] who specializes in [specialization area]. I have a [type of document] concerning [subject matter] which needs to be simplified for [target audience's] understanding without losing any critical information. Please guide me through the process of [main task], ensuring [key quality 1] and [key quality 2]. Illustrate your method with examples and break it down step by step, providing a clear pathway to achieve [desired outcome].

Examples

1. Act as a technical writer adept in breaking down complex legal terminology. I have a contract agreement concerning a business partnership which needs to be simplified for the stakeholders' understanding without losing any critical information. Please guide me through the process of making this agreement accessible, ensuring clarity and accuracy. Illustrate your method with examples and break it down step by step, providing a clear pathway to achieve a reader-friendly version of the agreement.
2. Act as a technical writer with a specialty in decoding intricate technical jargon. I have a software documentation concerning a new application's functionality which needs to be simplified for the end-users' understanding without losing any critical information. Please guide me through the process of rewriting this documentation into simpler terms, ensuring clarity and precision. Illustrate your method with examples and break it down step by step, providing a clear pathway to achieve a user-friendly version of the documentation.

PROMPT No. 126

To craft a compelling, relevant, and engaging speech within the specified time frame on the given topic for the targeted audience with the goal of inspiring, educating, or motivating them.

Prompt

Assume the role of a **motivational speaker** specializing in **career growth for young professionals**. Could you please craft a compelling **15**-minute speech on **"Embracing Failure to Fuel Success"** for an upcoming **conference of aspiring entrepreneurs**? Focus on **real-life examples, actionable insights, and that inspires courage and resilience**. Write using an **energetic** tone and a **dynamic** writing style. Let's ignite passion and purpose

Formula

Assume the role of a **[profession]** specializing in **[area/topic]**. Could you please craft a compelling **[length]**-minute speech on **"[Title]"** for an upcoming **[event/type of audience]**? Focus on **[types of content]**. Write using a **[tone]** and **[style]** writing style. Let's ignite passion and purpose

Examples

1. Assume the role of a TEDx speaker specializing in personal branding for freelancers. Could you draft a compelling 10-minute talk on "Leveraging Your Unique Skills in the Gig Economy" for an upcoming gig worker summit? Prioritize case studies, practical tips, and a tone that motivates and enlightens. Write using a passionate tone and an engaging writing style. Let's empower freelancers for success.
2. Assume the role of a mindfulness coach specializing in work-life balance. Could you design a transformative 20-minute workshop on "The Art of Mindful Productivity" for an annual corporate retreat? Concentrate on practical exercises, scientific findings, and a tone that fosters tranquility and focus. Write using a calming tone and an instructive writing style. Let's cultivate mindfulness and efficiency.

PROMPT No. 127

Goal

To analyze the practices, strategies, and behaviors of top performers in a specific field and extract valuable lessons that can be applied to your life.

Prompt

Assume the role of a **brand expert** specializing in **online professional branding for executives in the energy industry**. Could you conduct an analysis of **leading performers** on **LinkedIn in this field** and compile a list of key lessons that can be learned from their p**ractices, strategies, and behaviors**? The aim is to **significantly enhance my brand image on LinkedIn**. Write using a **positive** tone and a **constructive writing** style.

Formula

Assume the role of a **[profession]** specializing in **[area/topic]**. Could you conduct an analysis of **[target group]** on **[platform/venue]** and compile a list of key lessons that can be learned from their **[specific activities/behaviors]**? The aim is to **[desired outcome]**. Write using a **[tone]** and **[style]** writing style.

Examples

1. Assume the role of a social media consultant specializing in personal branding for academics. Could you perform a study on successful academics in the field of psychology on Twitter and compile insights that could be gained from their content strategy, posting frequency, and engagement tactics? The objective is to elevate my professional presence on Twitter. Write using an informative tone and a detailed writing style.
2. Assume the role of a marketing analyst focusing on online branding for small business owners in the retail sector. Could you evaluate the top-performing small businesses on Instagram and draw key lessons from their visual aesthetics, caption strategies, and hashtag usage? The goal is to boost my business' brand visibility on Instagram. Write using an encouraging tone and an actionable writing style.

PROMPT No. 128

Goal

To generate a list of engaging and attention-grabbing blog post titles related to a specific topic. The titles should be catchy and compelling, enticing readers to click and read the blog post.

Prompt

Act as a **copywriter** specializing in **marketing** for **entrepreneurs**.
I am currently working on a blog post discussing **"Digital Marketing Strategies for Small Businesses"**. However, I'm having difficulty brainstorming a captivating title. I would appreciate it if you could offer 5 suggestions for a blog title that will pique readers' interest and entice them to click. Provide very creative and overlooked suggestions. Write using a **positive** tone and **informative** writing style.

Formula

Act as a **[profession]** specializing in **[topic]** for **[profession]**. I am currently working on a blog post discussing **[subject/topic]**. However, I'm having difficulty brainstorming a captivating title. I would appreciate it if you could offer 5 suggestions for a blog title that will pique readers' interest and entice them to click. Provide very creative and overlooked suggestions. Write using a **[type]** tone and **[style]** writing style.

Examples

1. Act as a professional writer specializing in productivity improvement for finance professionals]. I am currently working on a blog post discussing "Innovative Ways to Boost Employee Productivity". However, I'm having difficulty brainstorming a captivating title. I would appreciate it if you could offer 5 suggestions for a blog title that will pique readers' interest and entice them to click. Provide very creative and overlooked suggestions. Write using a hopeful tone and critical writing style.
2. Act as an executive coach specializing in time management for senior leaders in the tech industry. I am currently working on a blog post discussing "Effective Study Habits for Busy Professionals". However, I'm having difficulty brainstorming a captivating title. I would appreciate it if you could offer 5 suggestions for a blog title that will pique readers' interest and entice them to click. Provide very creative and overlooked suggestions. Write using an authoritative tone and descriptive writing style.

PROMPT No. 129

To generate a comprehensive list of the pros and cons associated with a specific decision, enabling the individual to make an informed choice based on a balanced evaluation of the potential advantages and disadvantages.

Prompt

Act as a **job counselor** with a focus on **job search** for professionals in the **finance industry**. I am currently contemplating whether or not to **switch my job from the for-profit to the not-for-profit sector**. Please present me with a list of pros and cons, highlighting the advantages and disadvantages associated with this decision to facilitate an objective evaluation of the potential outcomes. Write using a motivated tone and creative writing style. Let's analyze this piece by piece.

Formula

Act as a **[profession]** with a focus on **[topic]** for professionals in the **[industry]**. I am currently contemplating whether or not to **[decision]**. Please present me with a list of pros and cons, highlighting the advantages and disadvantages associated with this decision to facilitate an objective evaluation of the potential outcomes. Write using a **motivated** tone and **creative** writing style. Let's analyze this piece by piece.

Examples

1. Act as a career coach with a focus on job transition for professionals in the manufacturing industry. I am currently contemplating whether or not to start my own business and leave my corporate job. Please present me with a list of pros and cons, highlighting the advantages and disadvantages associated with this decision to facilitate an objective evaluation of the potential outcomes. Write using a enthusiastic tone and creative writing style. Let's go through this systematically.

2. Act as a career development advisor with a focus on professional development for professionals in the capital market industry. I am currently contemplating whether or not to pursue further education. Please present me with a list of pros and cons, highlighting the advantages and disadvantages associated with this decision to facilitate an objective evaluation of the potential outcomes. Write using a motivated tone and persuasive writing style. Let's analyze this piece by piece.

PROMPT No. 130

Goal

To receive a comprehensive, step-by-step solution to a specific problem, along with clear instructions on how to execute each step.

Prompt

Assume the role of a **brand expert** specializing in p**ersonal branding for professionals in the food industry**. Provide me with a step-by-step solution to tackle the problem of **struggling to create a strong personal brand for myself**. Include clear instructions on how to execute each step effectively. Present a **thorough and extensive** set of recommendations, incorporating **unconventional ideas, resources, strategies, and tools**. Write using an **authoritative** tone and an **informative** writing style.

Formula

Assume the role of a **[profession]** specializing in **[area/topic]**. Provide me with a step-by-step solution to tackle the problem of **[challenge/problem]**. Include clear instructions on how to execute each step effectively. Present a **[depth descriptor]** and **[breadth descriptor]** set of recommendations, incorporating **[methods/technics]**. Write using a **[tone]** and **[style]** writing style.

1. Assume the role of a career coach specializing in career transitions for mid-level managers. Provide me with a step-by-step guide to manage the challenge of switching industries. Include explicit instructions for each step's successful implementation. Offer an in-depth and comprehensive set of suggestions, incorporating rare insights, unconventional methods, and lesser-known tools. Write using a confident tone and a guiding writing style.

2. Assume the role of a financial advisor with a focus on investment strategies for young professionals. Provide me with a step-by-step approach to tackle the problem of lacking a diversified investment portfolio. Furnish detailed steps for effective execution. Present a comprehensive and detailed set of strategies, including unconventional financial instruments, underused resources, and innovative methods. Write using a reassuring tone and an educational writing style.

PROMPT No. 131

Goal

To summarize long documents and articles

Prompt

Act as a **career analyst** specializing in **market trends** for professionals in the **tech industry**. Can you summarize **this lengthy report on emerging technologies and their impact on job opportunities**? Focus on **key findings, implications, and actionable insights**. Write using a **concise** tone and a **straightforward** writing style. Let's distill the essence of the information. Here is the content of the document: **[insert content]**

Formula

Act as a **[profession]** specializing in **[topic]** for **[industry/target audience]**. Can you summarize this **[type of document, e.g., report/article]** on **[subject]**? Focus on **[specific elements, e.g., key findings/implications/actionable insights]**. Write using a **[type]** tone and **[style]** writing style. Let's approach methodically/distill the essence of the information. Here is the content of the document: **[insert content]**

Examples

1. Act as a resume consultant specializing in executive-level professionals. Can you summarize this comprehensive guide on creating impactful executive resumes? Emphasize essential tips, common mistakes to avoid, and best practices. Write using an instructive tone and a reader-friendly writing style. Let's crystallize the key takeaways. Here is the content of the document: **[insert content]**
2. Act as a job market researcher with expertise in the healthcare sector. Can you condense this extensive article on the shifting demands for healthcare professionals during the post-pandemic era? Highlight trends, challenges, and opportunities. Write using an

informative tone and an analytical writing style. Let's capture the core insights. Here is the content of the document: **[insert content]**

PROMPT No. 132

Goal

To equip professionals with actionable prompts for developing and maintaining robust systems, addressing both common and emerging challenges, ensuring long-term resilience and effectiveness.

Prompt

Act as a **cybersecurity expert** specializing in **threat mitigation** for **small businesses**. I am seeking to provide a tailored set of **10** insightful prompts to **IT professionals** that will aid in the **effective development and ongoing maintenance of secure systems**. These prompts should cover both **common threats like phishing and malware, as well as emerging challenges such as ransomware attacks and supply chain vulnerabilities**. Employ an **analytical tone** and a **detail-oriented writing style** to elucidate each prompt, facilitating **a culture of heightened security awareness and proactive defense measures**. Through **collaborative intelligence, let's endeavor to fortify our security infrastructure against the evolving threat landscape**. Let's think about this step by step.

Formula

Act as a **[profession]** specializing in **[area of expertise]** for **[target audience]**. I am seeking to provide a tailored set of **[number]** insightful prompts to **[target professionals]** that will aid in the **[desired outcome]**. These prompts should cover both **[list of topics/challenges to be addressed]**. Employ a[n] **[specified tone]** and a **[specified writing style]** to elucidate each prompt, facilitating **[desired impact]**. Through **[a phrase encapsulating the broader objective]**. Let's think about this step by step.

Examples

1. Act as a network security analyst with a specialization in intrusion detection for educational institutions. I am looking to furnish a set of 5 pragmatic prompts to network administrators that will support the enhancement and continuous monitoring of intrusion detection systems. These prompts should delve into common network vulnerabilities like unauthorized access, as well as emerging challenges such as zero-day exploits. Adopt a problem-solving tone and a technical writing style to elaborate on each prompt, promoting a vigilant and responsive network security posture. Through shared cybersecurity acumen, let's aspire to safeguard our educational environments from unauthorized intrusions and potential data breaches. Let's think about this step by step.

2. Act as a data privacy consultant focusing on compliance for mid-size enterprises. I am aiming to deliver a precise set of 7 actionable prompts to legal teams that will assist in navigating the complex regulatory landscape, ensuring ongoing compliance with GDPR and other relevant data protection laws. These prompts should address both routine compliance monitoring and the implications of upcoming privacy legislation. Utilize a meticulous tone and a regulatory-centric writing style to expound on each prompt, fostering a culture of proactive legal adaptability and robust data governance. Through informed legal foresight, let's strive to uphold our commitment to data privacy and regulatory adherence. Let's think about this step by step.

PROMPT No. 133

Goal

To seek expert guidance in creating a well-structured 30-day learning plan that focuses on helping beginners learn and improve their skills in a specific area.

Prompt

Act as a **leadership coach** specializing in the **health care industry**. With a strong desire to acquire and excel in **time management skills**, I am requesting your assistance in crafting a detailed 30-day learning plan designed specifically for beginners. This plan should outline a step-by-step approach to **enable me to learn and enhance** my **time management skills** effectively. Let's address this point by point. Write using an **enthusiastic** tone and **instructive** writing style.

Formula

Act as a **[profession]** specializing in the **[industry]**. With a strong desire to acquire and excel in **[desired skill]**, I am requesting your assistance in crafting a detailed 30-day learning plan designed specifically for beginners. This plan should outline a step-by-step approach to **[objective/outcome]** my **[desired skill]** effectively. Let's address this point by point. Write using a **[type]** tone and **[style]** writing style.

Examples

1. Act as a learning coach specializing in the supply industry. With a strong desire to acquire and excel in emotional intelligence skills, I am requesting your assistance in crafting a detailed 30-day learning plan designed specifically for beginners. This plan should outline a step-by-step approach to enable me to learn and enhance my emotional intelligence effectively. Let's address this point by point. Write using an inspirational tone and assertive writing style.

2. Act as a professional development coach specializing in the renewable energy industry. With a strong desire to acquire and excel in problem-solving skills, I am requesting your assistance in crafting a detailed 30-day learning plan designed specifically for beginners. This plan should outline a step-by-step approach to enable me to learn and enhance my problem-solving skills effectively. Let's address this point by point. Write using a professional tone and instructive writing style.

PROMPT No. 134

To improve your writing by getting feedback

Prompt

Assume the role of a **copywriter** specializing in the **risk management industry**. **Proofread** the **text** I have provided and correct any **grammar and spelling mistakes**. Also, make suggestions that **will improve the clarity of my writing**. Deliver a **complete** and **meticulous** output.

Formula

Assume the role of a [**profession**] specializing in [**industry/area**]. [**Action**] the [**type of content**] I have provided and correct any [**specific issues**]. Also, make suggestions that will [**intended improvement**]. Deliver a [**descriptor**] and [**descriptor**] output.

Examples

1. Assume the role of a copywriter specializing in the healthcare industry. Review the article I have supplied and fix any typographical and syntactical errors. Additionally, offer suggestions that will enhance the readability of my article. Deliver a thorough and precise output.
2. Assume the role of a copywriter specializing in the finance sector. Examine the financial report I have submitted and amend any punctuation and formatting issues. Also, propose changes that will make the content more understandable for the reader. Deliver a comprehensive and accurate output.

PROMPT No. 135

Goal

To obtain guidance and actionable steps for your career-related dilemmas, based on how a chosen influential personality would likely approach and resolve similar situations.

Prompt

Act as a **leadership coach** specializing in **job transition** for professionals in the hospitality industry. If I find myself **stuck** in a career-related **dilemma**, how would **Satya Nadella** approach it? I want you to respond to this situation using the same mental models, thought processes, and tone that Satya Nadella would adopt. Plus, each answer should conclude with a practical step I can take to address my doubts. For the chosen personality, consider **Satya Nadella's strategic and humble approach as an immigrant from India** and my specific doubt is **how to navigate my career as an immigrant**. Present detailed and broad-ranging solutions. Let's address this point by point.

Formula

Act as a [**profession**] specializing in [**topic**] for professionals in the [**industry**]. If I find myself [**feelings/situation**] in a career-related [**dilemma/problem**], how would [**personality**] approach it? I want you to respond to this situation using the same mental models, thought processes, and tone that [**personality**] would adopt. Plus, each answer should conclude with a practical step I can take to address my doubts. For the chosen personality, consider [**personality details**] and my specific doubt is [**doubt details**]. Present detailed and broad-ranging answers. Let's address this point by point. Make sure to provide **[type of advice/resources]**. Write in a **[tone]** and **[style]** writing style.

1. Act as an executive search consultant specializing in job transition for professionals in the retail industry. If I find myself stuck in a career-related dilemma, how would Elon Musk approach it? I want you to respond to this situation using the same mental models, thought processes, and tone that Elon Musk would adopt. Plus, each answer should conclude with a practical step I can take to address my doubts. For the chosen personality, consider Elon Musk, an entrepreneur known for his risk-taking and visionary thinking, and my specific doubt is whether I should leave my stable job to start a new business. Present detailed and broad-ranging answers. Write in an informative and straightforward tone. Let's address this point by point.

2. Act as a LinkedIn career coach specializing in skills development for professionals in the tech industry. If I find myself struggling with a career-related challenge, how would Sheryl Sandberg approach it? I want you to respond to this situation using the same mental models, thought processes, and tone that Sheryl Sandberg would adopt. Plus, each answer should conclude with a practical step I can take to address my doubts. For the chosen personality, consider Sheryl Sandberg, former COO of Facebook known for her leadership and advocacy for women in business, and my specific doubt is how to navigate the corporate ladder as a woman. Present detailed and broad-ranging answers. Write in a supportive and clear tone. Let's take this one step at a time.

PROMPT No. 136

To provide tailored recommendations for online courses, resources, or certifications that can help you enhance your skills and qualifications aligned with career aspirations.

Act as a **financial advisor** specializing in **career transitions** for professionals in the **manufacturing industry**. Considering my **career goals** and current resume, could you suggest suitable **online courses, resources, or certifications** that I could engage with to enhance my skills and qualifications? Provide a comprehensive list of relevant online courses, resources, or certifications. Write using an **enthusiastic tone** and **creative writing style**. My career goals are **to become a team lead in the manufacturing industry** and my resume is: **[insert resume]**

Act as a **[profession]** specializing in **[topic]** for professionals in the **[industry]**. Considering my **[career goals/aspirations]** and current resume, could you suggest suitable **[training/online courses/resources/certifications]** that I could engage with to enhance my skills and qualifications? Provide a comprehensive list of relevant online courses, resources, or certifications. Write using a **[type]** tone and **[style]** writing style. My career goals are **[insert goals]** and my resume is: **[insert resume]**

1. Act as a career consultant specializing in career transitions for professionals in the insurance industry. Considering my career goals and current resume, could you suggest suitable online courses that I could engage with to enhance my skills and qualifications? Provide a

comprehensive list of relevant online courses. Write using an enthusiastic tone and creative writing style. My career goals are to work as an insurance broker with expertise in artificial intelligence in the insurance industry and my resume is: [insert resume]

2. Act as an employment coordinator specializing in e-commerce for professionals in the retail industry. Considering my career goals and current resume, could you suggest suitable training programs that I could engage with to enhance my skills and qualifications? Provide a comprehensive list of training programs. Write using an inspirational tone and academic writing style. My career goals are to develop my sales skills in the e-commerce industry and my resume is: [insert resume]

CONCLUSION

The journey of a job seeker, whether freshly embarking upon new horizons or seeking a change in direction, has often been equated to navigating uncharted waters. But as you've discovered in these pages, you are not left adrift without a compass. With the power of Generative AI and our meticulously crafted prompts, the vastness of the job market becomes a sea of opportunity, waiting to be harnessed.

We have journeyed together through over a hundred prompts, each designed to empower, to clarify, and to provide a sharper lens through which to view your own skills, passions, and aspirations. These are not mere tools, but keys—keys that can unlock doors, bridge gaps, and illuminate pathways that once seemed clouded in mystery.

Yet, our role as authors is not to provide a mere list, but to impart a mindset—a mindset where the unknown becomes the exciting, where challenges transform into adventures, and where the future is shaped by limitless potential.

For those of you who began this book with trepidation, we hope you now feel armed with a newfound sense of confidence and insight. To those seasoned in the ways of the job search, may these innovative tools rejuvenate your spirit and outlook. And for everyone, we offer additional resources, ensuring that this book remains a living guide, evolving alongside you and the ever-changing job landscape.

In closing, we want to emphasize that this journey is profoundly personal. Your aspirations, dreams, and goals are uniquely yours, but you're never truly alone in this quest. The essence of Generative AI is a testament to the collective human experience—built on our shared knowledge, hopes, and endeavors. It's a bridge between you and countless others who've walked similar paths, a silent whisper of encouragement in your ear.

The future is brimming with opportunity, and with these tools at your fingertips, you're not just prepared—you're empowered. As you turn this page and set forth, remember that each new day is a canvas, and you hold the brush.

Dream boldly. Seek passionately. And let the journey itself be the reward. Here's to your boundless future, and the many successes that await you. Go forth, and let the world marvel at your story.

FOR YOUR CONSIDERATION

As you close this book, could you spare a moment to leave a review?

Your insights are more than just feedback; they're a roadmap for others navigating the job market. By sharing your thoughts, you're not just recommending this book—you're empowering someone to land their dream job or make a meaningful career change.

Thank you for being a guiding light in someone else's journey.

Best wishes,

Vanessa & Mauricio

PS. To leave your kind review, please scan this QR code.

APPENDIXES

Appendix No 1

Sign-In to Chatbots

1,1. Chat GPT

Step 1: Visit ChatGPT on https://chat.openai.com/chat Click on "Sign Up" and then create your account.

Step 2: Verify your Account. You'd have to enter your details, verify your email and give an OTP you'll receive on your phone.

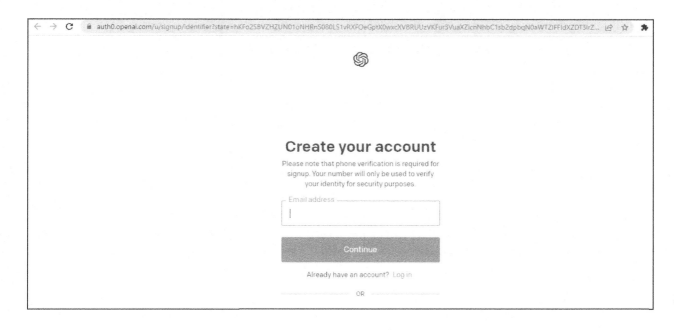

Once done, you'd have access to the free version of ChatGPT

As of April 2023, ChatGPT 3.5 is free to use and ChatGPT-4 costs $20 per month. As a beginner, you can easily test your skills on the free version.

This is how it looks:

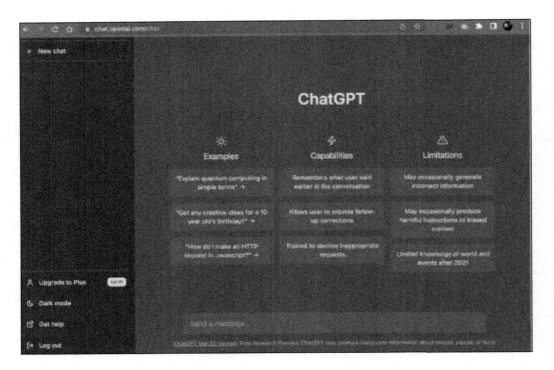

At the very bottom is where you'd chat:

You can now ask GPT anything you want, and it'll give you the desired result

Note: The procedure outlined was developed based on the instructions available at the time of writing. If you require further assistance with signing up for ChatGPT, please scan this QR code:

1.2. Bing Chat

Step 1: Go to the Microsoft website (www.microsoft.com).

Locate the download page for Edge or look for "Microsoft Edge" in the search bar. If you don't want to download Microsoft Edge, go directly to Step 6. For better results, we recommend using Microsoft Edge.

Step 2: Click the download button and choose the version that fits your system.

Step 3: Once downloaded, open the setup file.

Step 4: A User Account Control dialog box will appear – click "Yes" to grant permission.

The installation wizard will guide you through a series of prompts and options. Review them carefully.

Step 5: To open Microsfot Edge, press Win + R on the keyboard to open the Run window.

In the Open field, type "microsoft-edge:" and press Enter on the keyboard or click or tap OK. Microsoft Edge is now open.

Step 6: Head to bing.com/chat

Step 7: From the pop-up that appears, click 'Start chatting'

Step 8: Enter the email address for the Microsoft account you'd like to use and click 'Next'.

If you don't have one, click 'Create one!' just under the text box and follow the instructions. Enter your password when prompted and click Next. From the following screen, choose whether you'd like to stay signed in or not. Click 'Chat Now'

Step 9: Choose your conversation style. If you've never used it before, it's best to stick with 'More Balanced'

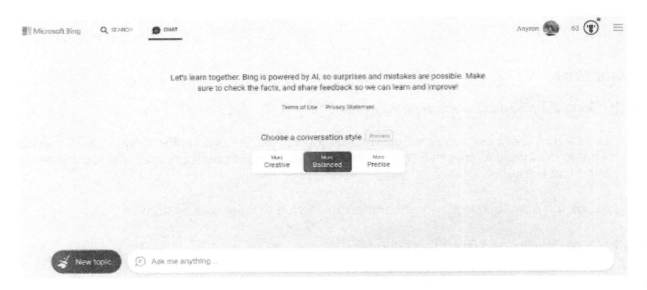

That's it! You can now start chatting.

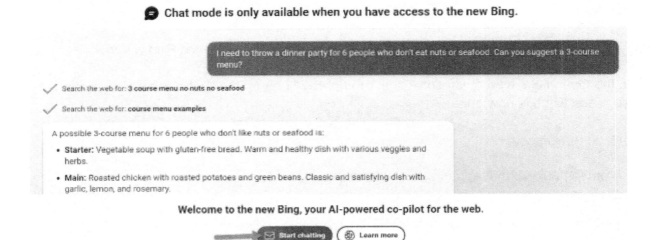

Note: The procedure outlined was developed based on the instructions available at the time of writing. If you require assistance with signing up for Bing Chat, please scan this QR code:

1.3. Google Bard

Step 1: Go to bard.google.com. Select Try Bard. Accept Google Bard Terms of Service

Step 2: Go to "Sign in"

Step 3: Enter a query or search term and then hit enter.

Wait for the AI to respond. You can then either continue the conversation or select Google It to use the traditional search engine.

Note: The procedure outlined was developed based on the instructions available at the time of writing. If you require assistance with signing up for Google Bard, please scan this QR code:

1.4. Meta LLaMA

Getting the Models

Step 1: Go to https://ai.meta.com/resources/models-and-libraries/llama-downloads/

Step 2: Fill the form with your information.

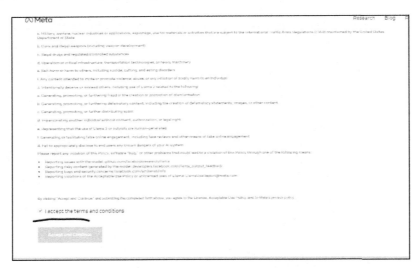

Step 3: Accept their license (if you agree with it)

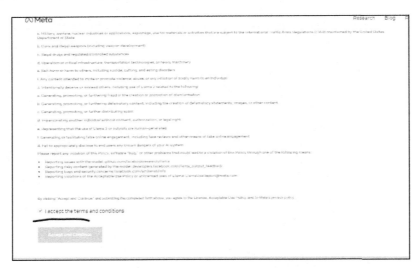

Step 4: Once your request is approved, you will receive a signed URL over email.

Step 5: Clone the Llama 2 repository (go to https://github.com/facebookresearch/llama).

Step 6: Run the download.sh script, passing the URL provided when prompted to start the download.

Keep in mind that the links expire after 24 hours and a certain amount of downloads. If you start seeing errors such as 403: Forbidden, you can always re-request a link.

Appendix No 2

Follow-up Prompts

There are 1100 prompts that you can use as follow-ups in order to get more specific or revised information from ChatGPT and other Chatbots. Don't forget to tailor these prompts to your specific circumstances and to the response you previously received from the Chatbot.

Each of these prompt types serves a different purpose and can be used effectively in different scenarios. Depending on the context and the intended outcome, one type of prompt may be more suitable than another.

These prompts are divided into eleven distinct categories, each tailored to specific conversational needs: Generic, Enhancement, Clarification, Probing, Critical Thinking, Instructional, Exploration, Comparison, Summarization, Evaluation, and Hypothetical.

To have access to 1100 follow-up prompts, please scan this QR code:

Appendix No 3

Free Resources

To get these FREE documents to help you with your job search, scan this QR code:

- Productivity Planner
- Brain Dump and Habit Tracker
- Company Website Logins
- Job Application Forms
- Job Search Planner

But if you want to purchase a paperback copy of the two books, scan the respective QR code:

- Productivity Planner, and
  Brain Dump and Habit Tracker

- Company Website Logins, Job Application
  Forms and Job Search Planner

Appendix No 4

ChatGPT Plugins

Enabling ChatGPT Plugins

If you have bought the paid version of ChatGPT, you'll have access to their plugins. OpenAI [the company that has built ChatGPT] has collaborated with many big companies to come up with plugins that make ChatGPT even more powerful. As of writing this Book, they have not made all plugins available to every user. However, very soon, you will be able to access them easily.

Once you buy the Pro Plan, you'll see two tabs like this on the top:

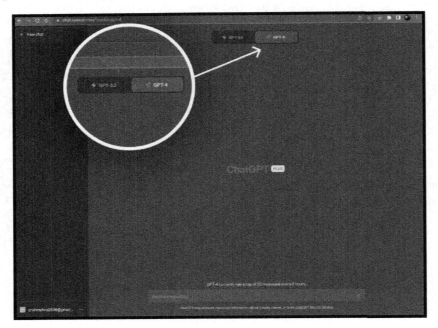

The difference in results is huge. The quality of results that you get from GPT-4 right now is way better than results from GPT 3.5. If **you can afford the paid plan, I would strongly recommend you to go for it.** However, you need a debit or credit card with International Payments enabled. You cannot use UPI to pay for this yet.

To enable plugins, you need to go to your Account Settings

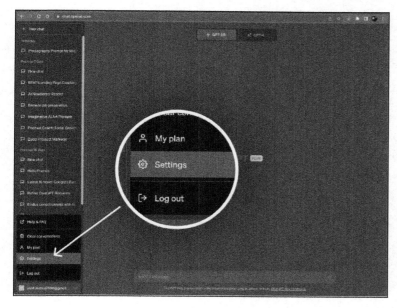

You can do a lot from this Settings Panel

- You can change the theme of your GPTK
- Clear all chats
- Enable/Disable plugins or internet access
- Enable/Disable history
- Export all your data.

Inside Settings, enable 'Browse with Bing' and 'Plugins'. If you cannot see this, cross check whether you have GPT Plus or not.

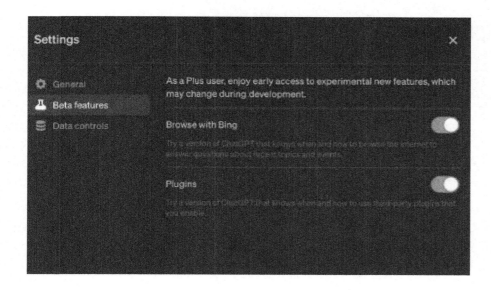

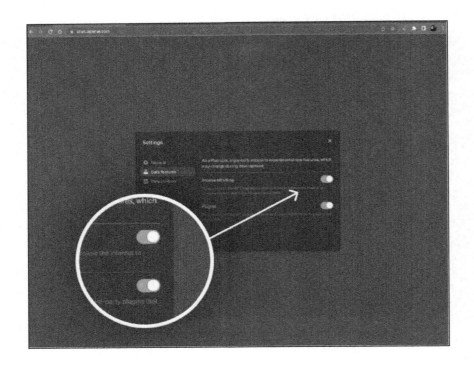

Once enabled, you'll see Plugins and Bing Browsing enabled under GPT-4.

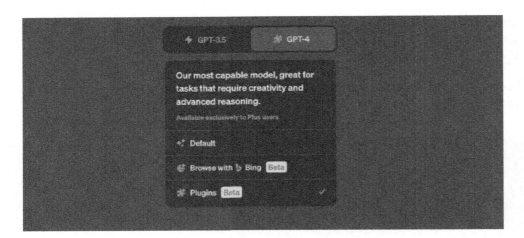

Great ChatGPT plugins to get a new job:

 Ambition
Install ↻

Search millions of jobs near you.

 AmazingTalker
Install ↻

Elevate your language learning at any level with personalized 1-on-1 online lessons from tutors across the world.

 Career Copilot
Install ↻

A trusted, always on assistant to help software developers find a better job. Built by Commit.dev.

 Easy Resume
Install ↻

Quickly create and edit your resume with the option to download as a dock or pdf, and find the job you deserve!

 edX
Install ↻

Find courses and content from leading universities to expand your knowledge at any level.

 KeyMate.AI Search
Install ↻

Search&Browse the web by using Google Search results with KeyMate.AI, your AI-powered web crawler.

 Link Reader
Install ↻

Reads the content of all kinds of links, like webpage, PDF, PPT, image, Word & other docs.

 Mindart
Install ↻

Career test to help you find your dream job, with automation risk and average salary.

 Video Insights
Install ↻

Interact with online video platforms like Youtube or Daily Motion.

 WebPilot
Install ↻

Browse & QA Webpage/PDF/Data. Generate articles, from one or more URLs.

Appendix No 5

Additional AI tools to Supercharge your Job Search

This section offers a curated list of external websites to augment your job search. While these resources are used, please note that we have no affiliation with them and cannot vouch for their reliability or accuracy. Exercise due diligence when using these platforms.

Jobscan [https://app.jobscan.co/] is one such tool that uses artificial intelligence and machine learning technology to give job seekers an instant analysis of how well their resume and cover letter are tailored for a particular job. The tool compares your resume with the job description and gives you a match score and issues that you can fix. Jobscan looks for keywords in the job description and compares them with your resume. The idea behind the tool is that if you add or modify your resume with the missing keywords, it will improve your match score and help you clear the ATS criteria.

Resume.io [https://resume.io/] is another useful tool that allows you to create a resume in a structured, easy-to-read format. It eliminates the need to edit resumes and fiddle around with tables and templates on Word or Google Documents. The free option allows you to choose one free template, but that should be enough to get you kickstarted. Once selected, you can modify your templates as many times as you want

Wonsulting [https://www.wonsulting.com/] is a service that provides resume consultation, but they also have free AI tools that anyone can use. Go to the website and navigate to wonsulting.ai. If you've spent years in a job and are struggling with reducing your experience to just a few lines, this AI is really useful. Just give it a prompt like "Led development of a project," and let it do its magic. It will give you three options that you can choose and modify. You get six free tokens, and each response consumes one token, so use them appropriately.

Resumaker.ai [https://resumaker.ai/] is a website that helps people make resumes in minutes. The portal provides users with several customizable, designer-made resume templates and intuitive tools to help them land their dream jobs. Unlike other resume builders, Resumaker.ai's artificial intelligence [AI] engine streamlines the resume-building process by automatically completing and filling in data for users. Resumaker.ai uses SSL encryption and other measures to safeguard user data against unauthorized access. You can use the tool's writing guides and recommendations to design a resume that stands out from the competition. Users can modify their resumes to reflect the requirements of the posted position, provide an overview of who they are, and utilize numbers to back up claims about their qualifications.

Aragon [https://www.aragon.ai/] is AI tool that lets users take polished headshots without visiting a photographer, spending time on hair and makeup, or waiting days for retouching. The user uploads 10 selfies, and the tool instantly returns 40 high-definition photographs. Moreover, the application protects users' privacy by encrypting data with AES256 and only storing it with service providers who have earned SOC 2 and ISO 27001 certifications. Please note that this service is not intended for use by anyone under the age of 18 since doing so is a violation of the terms of service.

Sonara.ai [https://www.sonara.ai/] Sonara is an innovative AI tool that revolutionizes the job search process by automating the tedious and time-consuming task of applying for jobs. By harnessing the power of artificial intelligence, Sonara combs through millions of job listings every day to identify and apply to relevant job openings on behalf of the user. Sonara takes the work out of finding a job by acting as your personal recruiter, leveraging AI and human expertise to represent you in the best possible light. Unlike traditional headhunters that cater exclusively to high-level executives, Sonara is accessible to job seekers at all levels.

JobScan [https://www.jobscan.co/] is one of the most popular resume optimization and job application platforms that tracks all the applied jobs from one place.Using the job tracker board, job seekers can create a list of jobs, optimize their resumes, and save interview schedules for all the ongoing applications.

Teal [https://www.tealhq.com/] is an all-in-one job application platform that offers rich features like a job application tracker, AI resume builder, and a career hub for students and job seekers. The tool creates a checklist for each job application, streamlining your queued job applications. Job seekers get recommendations based on the keywords from the job descriptions so that the resumes are tailored for the specific job.

Appendix No 6

A Beginner's Step-by-Step Guide to Using ChatGPT

If you're new to ChatGPT, don't fret. This guide is designed to walk you through its use, step by step. By the end, you'll have a solid grasp of how to harness the power of this incredible tool to aid in your job search and beyond.

Step 1: Accessing the Platform

Visit OpenAI's Platform: Head to OpenAI's official website: ChatGPT [openai.com]

Sign Up/Log In: If you don't have an account, you'll need to sign up. If you already have one, simply log in.

Step 2: Navigating the Interface

Dashboard: This is your central hub, where you can access various tools and see your usage stats.

Start a New Session: To interact with ChatGPT, start a new session or use a predefined platform depending on the current interface.

Step 3: Interacting with ChatGPT

Input Field: This is where you'll type or paste the prompts from our book.

Submit: Once you've entered your prompt, press 'Enter' or click the 'Submit' button.

Review Output: ChatGPT will generate a response. Take a moment to read and understand it.

Step 4: Refining Your Interaction

Being Specific: If you need specific information or a particular type of response, make your prompts more detailed.

Iterate: If the first response isn't what you're looking for, tweak your prompt and try again.

Step 5: Utilizing the Prompts from This Book

Choose a Prompt: Browse the book's prompt section and select one that aligns with your current job search needs.

Input: Copy and paste or type the chosen prompt into ChatGPT's input field.

Customization: Feel free to adjust the prompts to be more specific to your situation.

Step 6: Safety and Best Practices

Sensitive Information: Never share sensitive personal information, such as Social Security numbers or bank details, with ChatGPT or any online platform.

Understanding Outputs: Remember, while ChatGPT can produce human-like responses, it doesn't understand context in the same way humans do. Always review its advice with a critical eye.

Step 7: Exploring Advanced Features

As you become more comfortable with ChatGPT:

Experiment: Play around with different types of prompts to see the diverse responses you can get.

Integrate with Other Tools: There are several third-party tools and platforms that have integrated ChatGPT. Explore these to maximize your job search efforts.

Step 8: Stay Updated

Technology, especially in the AI field, evolves rapidly. Periodically check OpenAI's official channels for updates, new features, or changes to the platform.

By following this guide, even the most tech-averse individuals will find themselves comfortably navigating and interacting with ChatGPT. As we delve deeper into the book and introduce specific prompts tailored for job searching, you'll be equipped with the knowledge to make the most of them.

Here's to a more efficient, streamlined, and successful job search!

Appendix No 7

Unlock the Full Potential of This Book - Instantly

Dive into a world of convenience with our electronic copy! Feel free to seamlessly copy and paste any prompt that sparks your interest.

Customize them to fit your unique needs. Say goodbye to the hassle of retyping. Start crafting your perfect prompts with ease and efficiency!.

To access the electronic copy, please scan this QR code:

Printed in Great Britain
by Amazon

42581865R00084